Finding Light in the Darkness:
A Guide to Overcoming Anxiety and Depression

Mr. R. Dominguez, MIO-Psych

"Finding Light in the Darkness:
A Guide to Overcoming Anxiety and Depression"

Dedicatory:

To those on a profound journey towards psychological well-being, this book is dedicated with admiration and professional guidance. Within its pages, discover empowering insights and evidence-based strategies to transcend anxiety and depression. May your commitment to growth inspire resilience and a renewed sense of purpose. Embrace your authentic self and cultivate a life filled with joy and fulfillment.
With respect and belief in your journey,

Mr. Raul Dominguez, MIO-Psych

Embracing the Journey

In the depths of despair, when darkness engulfs our spirits, finding a flicker of light becomes our most cherished hope. Anxiety and depression, like formidable shadows, cast their influence over countless lives, dimming the vibrant colors of existence. However, within the human spirit resides an unwavering resilience, an indomitable spark that yearns to illuminate even the darkest corners of our souls.

Welcome to "Finding Light in the Darkness: A Guide to Overcoming Anxiety and Depression." Within these pages, we embark on a transformative journey, one that traverses the intricacies of anxiety and depression while empowering individuals to reclaim their inner radiance. Drawing from an array of insightful chapters, this guide illuminates the path to healing, offering guidance, solace, and practical tools to forge ahead.

Part I commences by providing a solid foundation, enabling a comprehensive understanding of anxiety and depression. We peel away the veils of mystery surrounding these conditions, unveiling their distinct characteristics and exploring the intricate connection between mind and body. By unraveling the underlying causes, we gain invaluable insights into the roots of our struggles.

With a deeper comprehension, Part II focuses on anxiety, dissecting its pervasive grip on our lives. We dismantle the anxiety spiral, revealing effective strategies to break free from its clutches. Through an exploration of various anxiety disorders, their symptoms, and signs, we strive to empower individuals with knowledge and self-awareness. By learning to tame the worry monster, we unveil newfound strength to confront and manage anxiety.

In Part III, we shift our focus to depression, shining a compassionate light on this insidious affliction. Through a comprehensive examination, we seek to understand the varied manifestations of depression, arming readers with the knowledge needed to recognize its presence. Navigating the dark days becomes a more manageable feat as we explore coping mechanisms and invaluable tools to combat depressive thoughts and behaviors.

Part IV is a beacon of hope, emphasizing healing and overcoming. By embracing the power of self-care, we embark on a journey of nurturing our minds, bodies, and spirits. We delve into therapeutic approaches, highlighting the importance of seeking professional help and exploring treatment options. Through the cultivation of resilience, we equip ourselves with the tools needed to triumph over adversity and embark on a path to long-term recovery.

As we ascend the peaks of personal growth, Part V paves the way for thriving beyond anxiety and depression. We shift our focus toward embracing positivity, cultivating joy, and expressing gratitude. Strengthening relationships becomes a vital component in our journey, as we discover the immense power of support and connection. Finally, we explore the profound meaning of a life well-lived, setting goals, and pursuing passions that infuse our existence with purpose and fulfillment.

"Finding Light in the Darkness: A Guide to Overcoming Anxiety and Depression" is more than just a book; it is a steadfast companion, providing solace and guidance to those navigating the labyrinth of anxiety and depression. Within its pages lies the collective wisdom, research, and experiences of countless individuals who have walked this path before. Together, let us embark on this transformative journey, where the quest for light becomes the catalyst for reclaiming our inner radiance.

Part I:
Understanding Anxiety and Depression

Demystifying Anxiety and Depression: Definitions and Overview

Unveiling the Veil of Mystery

In the realm of mental health, anxiety and depression often cloak themselves in an enigmatic veil, leaving many to grapple with confusion and misunderstanding. In this chapter, we embark on a journey to demystify anxiety and depression, shedding light on their true nature and offering a comprehensive overview.

Section 1: Understanding Anxiety

1.1 Defining Anxiety: Beyond Nervousness

Anxiety extends far beyond the realm of occasional nervousness. We delve into the intricacies of anxiety, exploring its multifaceted nature and its impact on daily life. By examining its physiological, cognitive, and emotional manifestations, we gain a deeper understanding of this pervasive condition.

1.2 The Anxiety Spectrum: Unraveling the Varieties

Anxiety encompasses a broad spectrum of experiences, ranging from generalized anxiety disorder (GAD) to panic disorder, social anxiety disorder, and specific phobias. We delve into each category, highlighting their unique features and shedding light on the common threads that bind them together.

1.3 Anxiety or Normal Worry: Discerning the Difference

Distinguishing between normal worry and clinical anxiety can be challenging. We explore the line between everyday concerns and anxiety disorders, equipping readers with tools to assess the severity, duration, and impact of their worries. By understanding this distinction, individuals can better navigate their own experiences.

Section 2: Exploring Depression

2.1 Unveiling Depression: Beyond Feeling Blue

Depression often hides beneath a facade, masquerading as mere sadness. We uncover the true nature of depression, unraveling the complexities that underlie this pervasive mental health condition. By exploring the emotional, cognitive, and physical symptoms, we dismantle the notion that depression is a fleeting or inconsequential experience.

2.2 Types of Depression: From Major Depressive Disorder to Dysthymia

Depression manifests in various forms, each with its own nuances and implications. We examine major depressive disorder (MDD), persistent depressive disorder (dysthymia), seasonal affective disorder (SAD), and postpartum depression, shedding light on their distinct characteristics. Through this exploration, readers gain insight into the diverse presentations of depression.

2.3 Demystifying the Dark Clouds: Causes and Triggers

Depression is often influenced by a multitude of factors, ranging from genetic predispositions to environmental stressors. We explore the underlying causes and triggers that contribute to the onset and persistence of depressive episodes. By uncovering these roots, we empower individuals to identify potential sources of their own struggles.

Section 3: Overlapping Pathways: Anxiety and Depression Interconnection

3.1 The Comorbidity Conundrum: Anxiety and Depression Hand in Hand

Anxiety and depression frequently coexist, intertwining their effects and complicating treatment approaches. We delve into the intricate relationship between these two conditions, examining the ways in which they reinforce and exacerbate one another. By recognizing their interconnectedness, individuals can develop a more comprehensive understanding of their own mental health experiences.

3.2 Shared Underlying Mechanisms: Neurobiology and Psychological Factors

Anxiety and depression share common neurobiological and psychological mechanisms. We explore the intricate workings of the brain, discussing the role of neurotransmitters, stress response systems, and cognitive processes in both conditions. Through this exploration, readers gain insight into the biological and psychological underpinnings of anxiety and depression.

3.3 Unraveling the Web: The Impact of Anxiety and Depression on Daily Life

Anxiety and depression cast their shadows over various facets of daily life, affecting relationships, work performance, and overall well-being. We shed light on the far-reaching consequences of these conditions, empowering individuals to recognize and address the impact of anxiety and depression on their daily lives. By understanding the ripple effects, individuals can seek appropriate support and develop strategies to mitigate the challenges they face.

Demystifying anxiety and depression is a crucial step in promoting understanding and fostering empathy for those navigating these conditions. By unraveling the definitions, exploring the nuances, and understanding the interconnected nature of anxiety and depression, we equip individuals with the knowledge to recognize and address their own experiences.

Through this comprehensive overview, we hope to create a foundation of understanding and empathy, breaking down the barriers that shroud anxiety and depression in mystery. By shedding light on these conditions, we empower individuals to seek support, cultivate self-care practices, and embark on a journey of healing and well-being.

Remember, you are not alone in your struggles. There is support available, and with understanding and compassion, we can work together to demystify anxiety and depression, fostering a world where mental health is destigmatized and every individual can thrive.

Once Upon a time,

In the bustling metropolis of modern life, where the cacophony of expectations and demands reverberates through the streets, there lived a woman named Emma. Behind her radiant smile and seemingly effortless grace, Emma bore the weight of anxiety and depression that cast a shadow over her every step. She yearned for a way out of the suffocating darkness that engulfed her spirit, a way to reclaim the vibrant essence of her being.

Emma's journey began as a fragile seed of self-awareness, planted during a moment of quiet contemplation amidst the chaos. In the depths of her despair, she made a choice, a solemn promise to herself, to embark on a quest for healing and liberation. With unwavering determination, she sought the guidance of mental health professionals, armed herself with knowledge, and embraced a resilience that would carry her through the darkest of days.

Through therapy sessions with Dr. Reyes, a compassionate psychologist with a profound understanding of the human psyche, Emma began to unravel the intricacies of her anxiety and depression. Dr. Reyes guided her gently through the labyrinthine corridors of her mind, helping her identify the underlying triggers and unhealed wounds that perpetuated her suffering. With each revelation, Emma gained a deeper understanding of herself, replacing self-judgment with compassion.

Emma discovered the transformative power of self-care, a ritualistic dance that nourished her mind, body, and spirit. She awakened each morning to the gentle embrace of meditation, setting intentions that would guide her through the day.

She indulged in the healing embrace of nature, taking long walks amidst sun-kissed meadows and finding solace in the symphony of rustling leaves. Through the language of art and creativity, she expressed her emotions, giving voice to her innermost thoughts and finding catharsis in the strokes of a paintbrush.

But Emma's journey was not without its trials. There were moments when anxiety and depression clutched at her heart with an iron grip, threatening to pull her back into the abyss. It was during these moments of despair that she sought the solace of support groups, where kindred souls shared their stories and lent strength to one another. In the warmth of their understanding, she found the courage to persevere, knowing that she was not alone in her struggles.

As Emma's journey unfolded, she began to rewrite the narrative of her life. She challenged the self-limiting beliefs that had held her captive and embraced a mindset of possibility and growth. With the guidance of books by esteemed psychologists like Dr. Carol Dweck and Dr. Martin Seligman, she learned to cultivate resilience and optimism, seeing setbacks as opportunities for learning and personal evolution.

Slowly but surely, the tendrils of healing crept into Emma's life, suffusing it with newfound purpose and joy. She rekindled old passions and pursued new interests, immersing herself in the richness of life's experiences. The love and support of her family and friends became beacons of light, guiding her through the darkest nights.

As Emma emerged from the depths of her own struggles, she became an advocate for mental health, a shining testament to the power of resilience and the capacity for transformation. She shared her story with unflinching honesty, encouraging others to seek help and offering a hand to those who felt lost in the labyrinth of anxiety and depression. Through her words and actions, she became a beacon of hope, illuminating the path for others to navigate their own journey towards healing and liberation. Emma's story serves as a powerful reminder that even in the darkest of times, there is light to be found. With unwavering determination, self-care, support, and a belief in the inherent strength within, anyone can transcend the suffocating grip of anxiety and depression. From the depths of her own journey, Emma emerged victorious, reclaiming her life and embracing a newfound sense of purpose and joy. Her story is a testament to the resilience of the human spirit, a reminder that there is always hope, even in the darkest of nights.

The Mind-Body Connection: How Anxiety and Depression Affect Your Well-being

The Ripple Effect of Anxiety and Depression

Anxiety and depression are not confined to the realm of thoughts and emotions; they have a profound impact on the intricate web of connections between the mind and the body. In this exploration of the mind-body connection, we unravel the intricate ways in which anxiety and depression affect your overall well-being, recognizing the profound interplay between mental and physical health.

Section 1: Physical Manifestations

1.1 The Weight of Worry: Understanding the Physical Symptoms of Anxiety

Anxiety can manifest itself in a multitude of physical symptoms. From rapid heartbeats and shallow breathing to muscle tension and digestive disturbances, anxiety takes a toll on the body. We delve into these physiological responses, shedding light on the profound impact of anxiety on your physical well-being.

1.2 The Weight of Sadness: Exploring the Physical Toll of Depression

Depression, too, leaves its mark on the body. We delve into the physical manifestations of depression, such as fatigue, changes in appetite and sleep patterns, and a weakened immune system. By understanding the physical toll of depression, we gain insight into the ways in which it affects overall well-being.

1.3 The Vicious Cycle: How Physical Symptoms Fuel Emotional Distress

The physical symptoms of anxiety and depression are not isolated experiences; they contribute to the emotional distress and perpetuate the cycle of mental health challenges. We explore the interconnected nature of physical and emotional symptoms, highlighting how they reinforce and intensify each other.

Section 2: Cognitive Impact

2.1 Racing Thoughts and Mental Fog: Anxiety's Influence on Cognitive Functioning

Anxiety disrupts cognitive processes, leading to racing thoughts, difficulty concentrating, and memory problems. We delve into the cognitive impact of anxiety, shedding light on how it affects your ability to think clearly, make decisions, and perform daily tasks effectively.

2.2 Foggy Horizons: Depression's Cloud Over Cognitive Abilities

Depression casts a fog over cognitive functioning, impairing concentration, memory, and decision-making. We explore the cognitive symptoms of depression, offering insights into the ways in which it affects your ability to engage with the world around you and find clarity in your thoughts.

2.3 The Cycle of Negative Thinking: How Cognitive Impact Fuels Emotional Distress

The cognitive impact of anxiety and depression fuels a cycle of negative thinking and emotional distress. We examine the ways in which distorted thinking patterns and cognitive biases contribute to the perpetuation of anxiety and depression. By recognizing these patterns, we empower individuals to challenge negative thoughts and cultivate more adaptive thinking styles.

Section 3: Emotion and Energy

3.1 The Emotional Roller Coaster: Anxiety's Influence on Mood

Anxiety takes a toll on your emotional well-being, leading to heightened irritability, restlessness, and a constant sense of unease. We explore the emotional impact of anxiety, offering insights into the ways in which it colors your experiences and affects your overall mood.

3.2 The Weight of Despair: Depression's Shadow on Emotional Well-being

Depression envelops you in a cloud of sadness, numbing your emotions and diminishing your capacity for joy. We delve into the emotional impact of depression, shedding light on the feelings of hopelessness, emptiness, and sadness that accompany this condition. By understanding the emotional toll of depression, we foster empathy and self-compassion.

3.3 The Energy Drain: How Emotional Distress Impacts Physical Vitality

Anxiety and depression drain your energy reserves, leaving you feeling fatigued, lethargic, and devoid of motivation. We explore the ways in which emotional distress affects your physical vitality, examining the intricate interplay between mental and physical energy. By recognizing this connection, we can gain insight into how anxiety and depression impact your overall well-being.

Nurturing Balance: Restoring the Mind-Body Connection

Section 1: Holistic Approaches

1.1 Mindfulness and Meditation: Cultivating Present-Moment Awareness

Practices such as mindfulness and meditation offer tools to reconnect the mind and body. We explore these techniques, highlighting their ability to reduce anxiety, alleviate depressive symptoms, and promote overall well-being. By incorporating mindfulness into your daily life, you can cultivate a deeper awareness of the mind-body connection.

1.2 Exercise and Movement: Energizing the Body and Mind

Physical activity is a powerful tool in restoring balance to the mind and body. We discuss the benefits of exercise in managing anxiety and depression, including its ability to release endorphins, improve sleep quality, and enhance mood. By incorporating regular movement into your routine, you can harness the transformative power of physical activity.

1.3 Nutrition and Well-being: Fueling the Body for Mental Health

The food we consume plays a significant role in our mental well-being. We explore the connection between nutrition and anxiety/depression, discussing the impact of certain nutrients on brain function and mood regulation. By adopting a balanced and nourishing diet, you can support the mind-body connection and enhance your overall well-being.

Section 2: Self-Care Practices

2.1 Restorative Sleep: Rejuvenating the Mind and Body

Quality sleep is essential for maintaining optimal mental health. We delve into the importance of establishing healthy sleep habits and explore strategies for improving sleep quality. By prioritizing restorative sleep, you can promote the restoration of the mind-body connection and enhance your resilience against anxiety and depression.

2.2 Stress Reduction Techniques: Calming the Mind, Soothing the Body

Stress is a significant contributor to anxiety and depression. We explore various stress reduction techniques, such as deep breathing exercises, progressive muscle relaxation, and journaling. By incorporating these practices into your daily routine, you can mitigate the impact of stress on your well-being and nurture the mind-body connection.

2.3 Self-Compassion and Emotional Well-being: Cultivating Inner Kindness

Self-compassion is a transformative practice that allows us to extend kindness and understanding to ourselves. We delve into the power of self-compassion in managing anxiety and depression, emphasizing the importance of self-care and self-acceptance. By cultivating a compassionate mindset, you can foster a stronger mind-body connection and support your emotional well-being.

Section 3: Seeking Professional Support

3.1 Therapy and Counseling: Navigating the Path to Healing

Professional support is instrumental in restoring the mind-body connection. We discuss various therapeutic approaches, such as cognitive-behavioral therapy (CBT), mindfulness-based therapy, and psychodynamic therapy. By seeking the guidance of a mental health professional, you can receive personalized support and gain valuable insights to overcome anxiety and depression.

3.2 Medication and Psychopharmacology: Balancing Neurochemicals

In some cases, medication may be necessary to restore the balance of neurochemicals in the brain. We explore the role of medication in managing anxiety and depression, highlighting the importance of working closely with a healthcare provider to determine the most appropriate treatment plan. By integrating medication when needed, you can support the mind-body connection and facilitate your journey toward well-being.

Embracing Wholeness: Integrating the Mind and Body

Section 1: Developing Mindful Awareness

1.1 Cultivating Mindfulness in Everyday Life

Mindfulness is more than a practice; it is a way of living. We explore how you can infuse mindfulness into your daily activities, fostering a deeper connection between your mind and body. By bringing awareness to the present moment, you can cultivate a sense of wholeness and align your mind and body.

1.2 Embracing Mind-Body Practices

We delve into additional mind-body practices that promote integration and well-being. These may include yoga, tai chi, qigong, and other movement-based modalities that foster a harmonious connection between the mind and body. By engaging in these practices, you can enhance self-awareness, reduce stress, and promote overall balance.

Section 2: Creating a Supportive Environment

2.1 Cultivating Healthy Relationships

Healthy relationships provide a nurturing environment for the mind-body connection to thrive. We explore the importance of building strong social connections, setting boundaries, and seeking support from loved ones. By fostering meaningful relationships, you create a support network that promotes emotional well-being and facilitates the healing process.

2.2 Creating a Sanctuary: The Importance of Physical Space

Our physical environment plays a significant role in our overall well-being. We discuss the significance of creating a sanctuary within your living space–a place that promotes relaxation, tranquility, and positivity. By curating a supportive physical environment, you provide a foundation for the mind-body connection to flourish.

Section 3: Cultivating Resilience and Growth

3.1 Embracing Mindful Resilience

Resilience is the capacity to bounce back from adversity. We explore the concept of mindful resilience, which involves cultivating a growth mindset, practicing self-compassion, and embracing the lessons learned from challenges. By nurturing resilience, you can navigate the ups and downs of life with greater ease, promoting the integration of your mind and body.

3.2 Tapping into Your Inner Strengths

Each individual possesses unique strengths and inner resources. We delve into techniques for identifying and harnessing these strengths, such as gratitude practices, affirmations, and visualization exercises. By tapping into your inner reservoir of strength, you bolster your mind-body connection and empower yourself on your journey toward well-being.

Sustaining the Mind-Body Connection: A Lifelong Journey

Section 1: Daily Mind-Body Rituals

1.1 Integrating Mind-Body Practices into Your Routine

We discuss the importance of integrating mind-body practices into your daily routine to sustain the mind-body connection. From morning rituals to evening self-care rituals, we explore various techniques for nourishing your mind and body consistently. By making these practices a priority, you foster a lasting sense of well-being.

1.2 Mindful Movement and Physical Activity

Physical movement and exercise continue to play a crucial role in maintaining the mind-body connection. We emphasize the significance of finding activities that bring you joy and incorporating them into your lifestyle. By engaging in mindful movement, you support your mental and physical health, strengthening the bond between your mind and body.

Section 2: Lifelong Learning and Growth

2.1 Committing to Personal Development

Continual learning and personal growth are essential components of sustaining the mind-body connection. We explore the value of seeking knowledge, engaging in self-reflection, and embracing new experiences. By committing to personal development, you expand your understanding of yourself and the world, fostering ongoing integration and well-being.

2.2 Cultivating Self-Compassion and Acceptance

Self-compassion and self-acceptance form the bedrock of sustaining the mind-body connection. We discuss the importance of treating yourself with kindness, embracing imperfections, and practicing forgiveness. By cultivating self-compassion and acceptance, you deepen your connection to yourself and nourish your overall well-being.

The mind-body connection is a profound and intricate relationship that shapes our well-being. As you navigate the challenges of anxiety and depression, remember that restoring and sustaining this connection is a lifelong journey. By embracing holistic

Unraveling the Causes: Exploring the Factors Behind Anxiety and Depression

Anxiety and depression are complex conditions that can impact individuals from all walks of life. While the experience of anxiety and depression may vary from person to person, it is crucial to understand the multitude of factors that can contribute to their development. In this chapter, we embark on a journey to unravel the causes of anxiety and depression, exploring the intricate interplay of biological, psychological, and environmental factors.

Section 1: Biological Factors

1.1 Genetic Predisposition: The Influence of Inherited Traits

Research suggests that genetics can play a role in the development of anxiety and depression. We delve into the impact of genetic predisposition, examining how certain genes and hereditary factors can increase the likelihood of experiencing these conditions. By understanding the genetic component, individuals can gain insight into their own vulnerabilities and seek appropriate support.

1.2 Neurochemical Imbalances: Disruptions in Brain Chemistry

The brain's delicate balance of neurotransmitters, such as serotonin, dopamine, and norepinephrine, plays a significant role in regulating mood and emotions. We explore the link between neurochemical imbalances and anxiety and depression, highlighting the potential impact of these disruptions on mental well-being. Understanding the neurobiological factors at play can inform treatment approaches and interventions.

1.3 Hormonal Factors: The Influence of Endocrine System

Hormones, such as cortisol and estrogen, can influence mood and emotional states. We examine the role of hormonal fluctuations, particularly during periods such as puberty, pregnancy, and menopause, in contributing to the onset or exacerbation of anxiety and depression. By recognizing the impact of hormonal factors, individuals can better navigate the potential challenges and seek appropriate support.

Section 2: Psychological and Emotional Factors

2.1 Cognitive Patterns: Unraveling Negative Thinking

Our thought patterns and cognitive processes can significantly influence our mental well-being. We explore the role of cognitive distortions, negative thinking patterns, and self-defeating beliefs in perpetuating anxiety and depression. By gaining awareness of these psychological factors, individuals can develop strategies to challenge and reframe unhelpful thoughts, fostering healthier mental states.

2.2 Trauma and Adverse Life Events: Navigating Past Wounds

Experiences of trauma and adverse life events can leave lasting imprints on our mental and emotional health. We examine the impact of traumatic experiences, such as abuse, loss, or significant life transitions, in triggering or exacerbating anxiety and depression. By addressing past wounds through therapy and self-care, individuals can begin the healing process and mitigate the effects of trauma on their mental well-being.

2.3 Personality Traits and Coping Mechanisms: Exploring Individual Differences

Each individual possesses unique personality traits and coping mechanisms that can influence their vulnerability to anxiety and depression. We delve into the connection between certain personality traits, such as perfectionism or high sensitivity, and their association with these conditions. By understanding individual differences, individuals can tailor their self-care practices and seek interventions that align with their specific needs.

Section 3: Environmental Factors

3.1 Family Dynamics and Childhood Experiences: Early Roots of Mental Health

Family dynamics and childhood experiences can shape our psychological well-being. We explore the impact of familial relationships, parenting styles, and childhood adversity on the development of anxiety and depression. By gaining insight into these environmental factors, individuals can recognize and address potential sources of distress and seek healing within their family systems.

3.2 Social Factors: The Influence of Social Support and Stigma

Our social connections, support networks, and societal attitudes toward mental health can significantly impact our well-being. We examine the role of social factors, such as social support, isolation, and stigma, in relation to anxiety and depression. By fostering positive social interactions, seeking supportive relationships, and challenging societal stigma, individuals can create an environment conducive to mental well-being.

3.3 Cultural and Socioeconomic Factors: Contextual Influences

Culture and socioeconomic factors shape our experiences and can contribute to the development of anxiety and depression. We explore how cultural norms, societal expectations, and socioeconomic disparities can impact mental health outcomes. By acknowledging the contextual influences, individuals can better understand the intersectionality of their experiences and work toward addressing systemic barriers to mental well-being.

Unraveling the causes of anxiety and depression requires a holistic perspective that acknowledges the interplay of biological, psychological, and environmental factors. By understanding the complex web of influences, individuals can gain insight into their own experiences and make informed decisions about their mental health.

It is important to remember that the causes of anxiety and depression are multifaceted and unique to each individual. While certain factors may contribute to their development, it is the interplay and combination of these factors that shapes our experiences. Therefore, a comprehensive approach to addressing anxiety and depression involves tailored interventions, such as therapy, medication, lifestyle changes, and self-care practices.

By unraveling the causes of anxiety and depression, we empower individuals to take an active role in their mental well-being. Recognizing the factors at play provides a roadmap for understanding, compassion, and effective intervention. It is through this understanding that we can dismantle stigma, promote early intervention, and create a supportive society that fosters the mental health of all individuals.

Remember, seeking support from mental health professionals, engaging in self-care practices, and building a strong support network are vital steps toward navigating the complexities of anxiety and depression. Together, we can unravel the causes, demystify these conditions, and work toward a world where mental health is prioritized, understood, and nurtured.

Part II: Shedding Light on Anxiety

In the realm of human emotions, anxiety is an intricate and pervasive force that affects individuals across cultures and ages. It is an inner turmoil that can cripple the mind and body, often casting a shadow on even the simplest of daily activities. Yet, amidst the complexity and prevalence of anxiety, there remains a glimmer of hope–a pursuit to understand and unravel its enigmatic nature.

Welcome to Part II of our exploration, where we delve deep into the multifaceted realm of anxiety, shedding light on its origins, manifestations, and the countless ways it intertwines with our lives. In this endeavor, we embark on a journey that aims to demystify anxiety, empowering us with knowledge and tools to navigate its intricate web.

Anxiety, at its core, is an inherent part of the human experience. From the pangs of anticipation before a major life event to the nagging worries that haunt our thoughts during uncertain times, anxiety is a universal phenomenon that transcends boundaries. However, it is crucial to distinguish between the occasional bouts of worry that accompany life's challenges and the clinical condition known as anxiety disorders, which can have a profound impact on an individual's well-being.

To fully comprehend anxiety, we must delve into its multifaceted nature, understanding its origins, triggers, and the intricate interplay between biological, psychological, and environmental factors. With advancements in scientific research and a deeper understanding of the human mind, we are gradually unraveling the complex tapestry of anxiety. Through Part II of our journey, we aim to present an in-depth exploration of anxiety, combining scientific insights, personal narratives, and practical strategies that can help individuals navigate this intricate terrain.

Within these pages, you will find an array of topics that span the spectrum of anxiety-related phenomena. We will venture into the realms of Generalized Anxiety Disorder (GAD), Panic Disorder, Social Anxiety Disorder, and more, unraveling their unique characteristics and offering guidance on how to recognize and address them. Moreover, we will explore the often-overlooked aspects of anxiety, such as the impact of cultural influences, societal pressures, and the role of technology in shaping our anxious landscapes.

However, our journey is not merely a clinical examination of anxiety; it is a testament to the resilience and strength of the human spirit. We will shine a light on the remarkable stories of individuals who have grappled with anxiety, triumphed over adversity, and found solace in various coping mechanisms. Through their narratives, we hope to inspire and empower others who may be caught in the clutches of anxiety, letting them know they are not alone on their journey towards healing.

It is important to note that while this exploration of anxiety is comprehensive, it is by no means exhaustive. Each person's experience with anxiety is unique, and there is no one-size-fits-all solution. Instead, we offer a tapestry of knowledge, insights, and practical advice that readers can draw upon, adapting and incorporating what resonates with their individual needs and circumstances.

So, let us embark on this transformative voyage together, seeking to understand anxiety in all its complexity. As we shed light on the shadows that anxiety casts, may we find comfort in the shared knowledge that we are not alone in our struggles. With compassion, understanding, and a commitment to fostering mental well-being, we can navigate the labyrinthine paths of anxiety, emerging stronger, wiser, and ready to embrace a life that is not defined by fear but enriched by resilience and hope.

The Anxiety Spiral: Breaking Free from its Grip

In the depths of anxiety lies an intricate and relentless force that can envelop our thoughts, emotions, and actions, creating a seemingly never-ending cycle of distress. It is this cycle, known as the Anxiety Spiral, that traps countless individuals in its grip, rendering them captive to their fears and worries. Yet, even in the face of this overwhelming challenge, there is hope—a path to liberation from the clutches of anxiety.

Welcome to an exploration of the Anxiety Spiral, a journey that aims to unravel the intricacies of this debilitating phenomenon, empowering individuals with knowledge and strategies to break free from its relentless grip. In this undertaking, we delve into the intricacies of the Anxiety Spiral, dissecting its origins, manifestations, and the various ways it affects our lives. By shedding light on this complex phenomenon, we seek to equip individuals with the tools necessary to overcome anxiety and forge a path towards healing.

At its core, the Anxiety Spiral represents a cyclical pattern of anxious thoughts, feelings, and behaviors that intensify over time. It often begins with a trigger—a specific event, a distressing thought, or a challenging situation that sets off a chain reaction within our minds. From there, anxiety takes hold, fueling a cascade of thoughts characterized by worry, fear, and anticipation of negative outcomes. These thoughts, in turn, amplify the emotional distress, further intensifying the anxiety we experience.

As the Anxiety Spiral gains momentum, it engulfs us in its grasp, influencing our behaviors and actions. We may find ourselves engaging in avoidance tactics, seeking to escape the discomfort anxiety brings. We might withdraw from social interactions, avoid situations that trigger anxiety, or even develop rituals and compulsions to temporarily alleviate our distress. However, these coping mechanisms often perpetuate the cycle, reinforcing anxiety's hold over us and deepening our sense of helplessness.

To break free from the Anxiety Spiral, it is essential to understand its underlying mechanisms and adopt a multifaceted approach towards healing. Through this exploration, we will traverse a diverse range of topics, examining the impact of cognitive distortions and negative thinking patterns on the spiral's perpetuation. We will delve into the interconnectedness of anxiety and physiological responses, exploring the intricate relationship between stress hormones, the nervous system, and the anxious mind.

Moreover, we will examine the influence of external factors on the Anxiety Spiral, recognizing the role of societal pressures, cultural expectations, and the relentless pace of modern life in fueling anxiety. By uncovering these external stressors, we can develop strategies to navigate and mitigate their impact, creating a more conducive environment for healing and growth.

Within these pages, we will encounter stories of individuals who have grappled with the Anxiety Spiral and emerged victorious. Their narratives serve as beacons of hope, illuminating the path towards breaking free from anxiety's grip. We will explore evidence-based techniques and therapies, such as cognitive-behavioral therapy, mindfulness practices, and self-compassion, which can help individuals interrupt the cycle and foster resilience.

It is important to acknowledge that the journey to breaking free from the Anxiety Spiral is not linear, nor does it adhere to a predetermined timeline. Each individual's experience with anxiety is unique, and the path to healing requires patience, self-compassion, and a willingness to seek support. This exploration serves as a guide, providing insights, tools, and encouragement to embark on the journey towards breaking free from anxiety's grip.

As we navigate the depths of the Anxiety Spiral together, let us remember that we are not alone. The shared experiences, knowledge, and support we encounter along the way provide solace and strength, reminding us that we are part of a larger community bound by our collective pursuit of well-being.

So, let us embark on this transformative journey together, stepping into the labyrinthine depths of the Anxiety Spiral with courage and determination. As we do so, we invite introspection and self-reflection, urging ourselves to confront the patterns and triggers that perpetuate the cycle.

One crucial aspect of breaking free from the Anxiety Spiral is developing a deep understanding of our thoughts and emotions. By cultivating awareness, we can recognize the distorted thinking patterns that feed into anxiety and challenge their validity. The power of reframing our thoughts and replacing negative self-talk with affirming and rational beliefs cannot be underestimated. It is through this process of cognitive restructuring that we can begin to unravel the tangled threads of the Anxiety Spiral, loosening its grip on our psyche.

Mindfulness, too, plays a pivotal role in our quest for liberation. By anchoring ourselves in the present moment, we can observe our anxious thoughts without judgment or attachment. Mindfulness empowers us to create space between our thoughts and our identities, allowing us to observe anxiety as a passing phenomenon rather than an intrinsic part of who we are. This newfound perspective becomes a cornerstone for breaking free from the Anxiety Spiral, fostering a sense of detachment and providing a refuge of calm amidst the storm.

In our pursuit of liberation, we must also recognize the significance of self-care and self-compassion. Nurturing our physical, emotional, and mental well-being is essential for building resilience and combating the grip of anxiety. Engaging in activities that bring us joy and peace, practicing relaxation techniques, and prioritizing restful sleep contribute to our overall sense of balance and equanimity. Moreover, extending compassion to ourselves during moments of distress and refraining from self-blame allows us to cultivate a kind and supportive inner dialogue that counteracts the negative self-judgment perpetuated by the Anxiety Spiral.

While self-reflection and individual practices are powerful, the journey towards breaking free from the Anxiety Spiral often benefits from the guidance and support of others. Seeking professional help, such as therapy or counseling, can provide invaluable tools, insights, and coping strategies tailored to our unique circumstances. Connecting with support groups or engaging in peer discussions allows us to draw strength from shared experiences and learn from the wisdom of others who have triumphed over anxiety's grasp. Remember, reaching out for support is not a sign of weakness, but an act of bravery and self-empowerment.

As we embark on this collective endeavor to break free from the Anxiety Spiral, let us also cultivate patience and perseverance. The journey may be marked by setbacks and challenges, but every step forward, no matter how small, is a testament to our resilience and commitment to reclaiming our lives from anxiety's clutches. It is through this unwavering dedication that we can gradually dismantle the Anxiety Spiral, forging a path towards liberation and embracing a life defined by courage, authenticity, and inner peace.

So, let us continue this transformative journey, hand in hand, as we unravel the intricacies of the Anxiety Spiral. Together, we will discover the power within ourselves to break free from its grip, paving the way for a future filled with hope, resilience, and a renewed sense of possibility.

Anxiety has a way of trapping individuals in a relentless cycle of worry, fear, and distress. This cycle, often referred to as the Anxiety Spiral, can be overwhelming and leave individuals feeling trapped and helpless. However, there is hope—a path to breaking free from its grip and reclaiming control over one's life.

The Anxiety Spiral is characterized by a repetitive pattern of anxious thoughts, emotions, and behaviors that intensify over time. It typically begins with a trigger, which could be a specific event, a distressing thought, or a challenging situation. This trigger sets off a chain reaction, where anxious thoughts start to dominate the individual's mind. These thoughts are often accompanied by a heightened sense of fear, worry, and anticipation of negative outcomes.

As the Anxiety Spiral gains momentum, it can lead to a range of physical and emotional symptoms. Individuals may experience increased heart rate, shortness of breath, muscle tension, restlessness, and difficulty concentrating. These symptoms further reinforce the anxious thoughts and perpetuate the cycle, creating a self-perpetuating feedback loop.

The Anxiety Spiral also influences behavior. In an attempt to alleviate distress, individuals may engage in avoidance strategies, such as avoiding certain situations or places that trigger anxiety. They may withdraw from social interactions or rely on rituals and compulsions to temporarily alleviate their anxiety. While these behaviors may provide temporary relief, they ultimately reinforce the cycle by preventing individuals from confronting and overcoming their fears.

Breaking free from the Anxiety Spiral requires a multifaceted approach that addresses the underlying causes and perpetuating factors. It begins with gaining a deeper understanding of one's own anxious thoughts and beliefs. Cognitive distortions, such as catastrophizing, overgeneralization, and black-and-white thinking, often contribute to the intensification of anxiety. By recognizing and challenging these distorted thoughts, individuals can reframe their thinking patterns and cultivate a more balanced and realistic perspective.

Practicing mindfulness is another powerful tool for breaking free from the Anxiety Spiral. Mindfulness involves intentionally bringing one's attention to the present moment without judgment. By cultivating a non-reactive awareness of anxious thoughts and emotions, individuals can create a mental space that allows them to observe their anxiety without getting entangled in it. Mindfulness practices, such as deep breathing, meditation, and body scans, help individuals develop a sense of grounding and reduce their reactivity to anxious thoughts.

Self-care and self-compassion are vital components of breaking free from the Anxiety Spiral. Engaging in activities that promote physical and emotional well-being, such as regular exercise, healthy eating, and sufficient sleep, can help reduce overall stress levels. Additionally, practicing self-compassion involves treating oneself with kindness, understanding, and acceptance in the face of anxiety. It means recognizing that anxiety is a common human experience and extending the same compassion to oneself as one would to a friend facing similar struggles.

Seeking professional help is also a crucial step in breaking free from the Anxiety Spiral. Therapists, counselors, or psychologists trained in treating anxiety disorders can provide valuable guidance, support, and evidence-based interventions.

Cognitive-behavioral therapy (CBT), for example, is a widely used therapeutic approach that helps individuals identify and challenge their anxious thoughts and behaviors. It equips individuals with practical strategies to change their response patterns and develop healthier coping mechanisms.

Building a support system is essential in the journey to break free from the Anxiety Spiral. Connecting with others who have experienced or are currently experiencing anxiety can provide a sense of validation, understanding, and encouragement. Support groups, online communities, or seeking out trusted friends and family members can offer a safe space to share experiences, exchange coping strategies, and receive empathetic support.

Breaking free from the Anxiety Spiral is not an overnight process. It requires commitment, patience, and perseverance. It is important to approach the journey with realistic expectations and an understanding that setbacks may occur. Healing takes time, and progress may come in small steps rather than leaps and bounds. Embracing patience and self-compassion throughout the process is crucial, as it allows individuals to be gentle with themselves and celebrate even the smallest victories.

In addition to individual efforts, creating a supportive environment is beneficial for breaking free from the Anxiety Spiral. This includes setting healthy boundaries, both in personal and professional relationships, and surrounding oneself with people who uplift and encourage personal growth. Engaging in open and honest communication about one's struggles with trusted individuals can foster understanding and empathy, cultivating a network of support that can help navigate the challenges of anxiety.

Another aspect of breaking free from the Anxiety Spiral is addressing any underlying factors contributing to anxiety. This may involve exploring past traumas, unresolved emotions, or deep-rooted belief systems that contribute to the perpetuation of anxious thoughts and behaviors. Seeking the assistance of a trained therapist or counselor can provide a safe space for processing these underlying issues and developing strategies for healing and growth.

It is important to note that breaking free from the Anxiety Spiral does not mean eliminating anxiety entirely. Anxiety is a natural human response, and it serves a protective function in certain situations. The goal is not to eradicate anxiety but rather to develop a healthier relationship with it. By cultivating resilience, coping mechanisms, and a supportive mindset, individuals can learn to manage anxiety in a way that allows them to live fulfilling and meaningful lives.

In the journey to break free from the Anxiety Spiral, it is essential to remember that progress is not linear. There may be ups and downs, moments of triumph and moments of struggle. It is during the challenging times that resilience is tested and growth is fostered. It is in these moments that individuals have the opportunity to practice the strategies they have learned, lean on their support system, and cultivate a sense of inner strength.

Ultimately, breaking free from the grip of the Anxiety Spiral is an empowering and transformative process. It requires a commitment to self-reflection, self-care, and self-compassion. By understanding the patterns and triggers that perpetuate anxiety, adopting evidence-based strategies, seeking support, and creating a nurturing environment, individuals can gradually loosen the grip of the Anxiety Spiral and reclaim their lives.

So, with courage and determination, let us embark on the journey of breaking free from the Anxiety Spiral. Let us embrace the challenges and celebrate the victories as we cultivate resilience, foster healing, and forge a path towards a life marked by freedom, peace, and empowered well-being.

Recognizing Anxiety Disorders: Types, Symptoms, and Signs

Anxiety is a natural response to stress, alerting us to potential threats and preparing our bodies to react. However, when anxiety becomes excessive, persistent, and interferes with daily life, it may be indicative of an anxiety disorder. These disorders are more than just occasional worries or nerves–they are complex mental health conditions that can significantly impact an individual's well-being and quality of life. Understanding the different types of anxiety disorders, their symptoms, and signs is crucial for accurate recognition and effective intervention.

Generalized Anxiety Disorder (GAD): Generalized Anxiety Disorder is characterized by excessive and uncontrollable worry about various aspects of life, such as work, relationships, health, or everyday situations. Individuals with GAD often find it challenging to control their worry, which may be accompanied by physical symptoms like restlessness, irritability, difficulty concentrating, muscle tension, and sleep disturbances. These symptoms persist for at least six months and can significantly impair daily functioning.

Panic Disorder: Panic Disorder involves recurrent and unexpected panic attacks, which are intense surges of fear or discomfort accompanied by physical symptoms like heart palpitations, chest pain, shortness of breath, dizziness, trembling, and a sense of impending doom. Panic attacks typically peak within minutes and can be so distressing that individuals may develop a fear of future attacks, leading to avoidance behaviors and agoraphobia.

Social Anxiety Disorder (Social Phobia): Social Anxiety Disorder is characterized by an intense fear of social situations or performance situations where individuals fear being judged, embarrassed, or humiliated. The fear of scrutiny can lead to avoidance of social interactions, resulting in significant distress and impairment in personal and professional relationships. Physical symptoms may include blushing, sweating, trembling, rapid heartbeat, and cognitive symptoms such as excessive self-consciousness and fear of being negatively evaluated.

Specific Phobias: Specific Phobias involve intense and irrational fears of specific objects, situations, or activities. Common examples include fear of heights, spiders, flying, needles, or enclosed spaces. When confronted with the phobic stimulus, individuals may experience extreme anxiety, panic attacks, and a strong desire to avoid the feared object or situation. Specific Phobias can significantly limit individuals' daily activities and cause distress.

Obsessive-Compulsive Disorder (OCD): Obsessive-Compulsive Disorder is characterized by intrusive, distressing thoughts (obsessions) and repetitive behaviors or mental acts (compulsions) aimed at reducing anxiety or preventing harm. Common obsessions revolve around themes of cleanliness, symmetry, or fear of harm, while compulsions often manifest as rituals or repetitive behaviors, such as excessive handwashing, checking, or counting. Individuals with OCD may experience significant distress and impairment due to the time-consuming nature of their rituals.

Post-Traumatic Stress Disorder (PTSD): Post-Traumatic Stress Disorder can develop after exposure to a traumatic event, such as a natural disaster, combat, physical or sexual assault, or witnessing a traumatic event. Symptoms may include intrusive memories, nightmares, flashbacks, avoidance of reminders associated with the trauma, emotional numbness, hyperarousal, hypervigilance, and changes in mood and cognition. PTSD can significantly impact an individual's daily functioning and quality of life.

Recognizing the signs and symptoms of anxiety disorders is crucial for early intervention and effective management. It is important to note that individuals may experience a combination of symptoms or exhibit symptoms from multiple anxiety disorders simultaneously. Additionally, anxiety disorders can coexist with other mental health conditions, such as depression, further complicating the diagnostic picture.

If you or someone you know is experiencing persistent and distressing anxiety symptoms that interfere with daily life, it is important to seek professional help from a qualified mental health professional. A thorough evaluation by a healthcare provider, such as a psychiatrist or psychologist, can lead to an accurate diagnosis and the development of a tailored treatment plan.

Treatment for anxiety disorders typically involves a combination of psychotherapy, medication, and self-help strategies. Cognitive-behavioral therapy (CBT) is a commonly used therapeutic approach that helps individuals identify and challenge negative thought patterns and develop healthy coping skills. Exposure therapy, a type of CBT, is often effective in treating specific phobias and PTSD, gradually exposing individuals to their feared objects or situations in a controlled and supportive environment.

Medications, such as selective serotonin reuptake inhibitors (SSRIs) or benzodiazepines, may be prescribed by a healthcare professional to manage symptoms of anxiety disorders. These medications can help alleviate symptoms and improve overall functioning. However, medication should be used under the guidance of a healthcare professional and is typically combined with therapy for optimal results.

In addition to professional treatment, individuals can also incorporate self-help strategies into their daily lives to manage anxiety. Regular exercise, practicing relaxation techniques such as deep breathing or mindfulness meditation, maintaining a healthy lifestyle with proper sleep and nutrition, and engaging in activities that bring joy and relaxation can all contribute to reducing anxiety symptoms.

Building a support network is crucial in managing anxiety disorders. Trusted friends, family members, or support groups can provide understanding, encouragement, and a safe space for individuals to share their experiences and challenges. Sharing experiences with others who have gone through similar struggles can provide a sense of validation and reduce feelings of isolation.

It is important to remember that recovery from anxiety disorders is a journey. Healing takes time, and it may involve setbacks along the way. Patience, self-compassion, and perseverance are key in navigating the challenges and working towards long-term management and well-being.

In conclusion, recognizing anxiety disorders involves understanding the different types, symptoms, and signs associated with these conditions. Early recognition and intervention are vital in effectively managing anxiety disorders and improving overall quality of life. Seeking professional help, developing a comprehensive treatment plan, and implementing self-help strategies are essential steps towards reclaiming control and living a fulfilling life free from the constraints of anxiety disorders. Remember, there is hope, and with the right support and resources, individuals can break free from the grip of anxiety and embark on a path of healing and recovery.

Taming the Worry Monster: Strategies for Managing Anxiety

Anxiety can often feel like a relentless, overpowering monster that consumes our thoughts, emotions, and daily lives. It manifests as excessive worry, fear, and unease, making it challenging to focus, relax, or engage in activities we once enjoyed. However, it's important to recognize that anxiety is something we can learn to manage and tame. By adopting effective strategies and tools, we can regain control over our lives and reduce the impact of the worry monster. Let's explore some practical strategies for managing anxiety.

1. **Understanding and Acceptance:**

The first step in managing anxiety is to develop an understanding of what anxiety is and accept that it is a normal part of the human experience. Anxiety is our body's response to perceived threats, but sometimes it becomes exaggerated or misaligned with reality. By acknowledging that anxiety is a common and natural response, we can reduce the power it holds over us.

2. **Deep Breathing and Relaxation Techniques:**

Deep breathing exercises and relaxation techniques are valuable tools for managing anxiety in the moment. When we experience anxiety, our breathing often becomes shallow and rapid, exacerbating the symptoms. By practicing deep breathing, we can activate the body's relaxation response, which helps calm the mind and reduce physiological symptoms. Techniques such as progressive muscle relaxation, guided imagery, and mindfulness meditation can also promote relaxation and reduce anxiety.

3. Challenging Negative Thoughts:

Anxiety is often fueled by negative thoughts and catastrophic thinking. Learning to challenge these thoughts and replace them with more realistic and positive ones is an important skill in managing anxiety. Cognitive-behavioral therapy (CBT) techniques can help identify and reframe irrational thoughts, enabling us to develop a more balanced perspective and reduce anxiety levels.

4. Time Management and Prioritization:

Anxiety can be exacerbated by feeling overwhelmed with tasks, responsibilities, and deadlines. Effective time management and prioritization techniques can help alleviate anxiety in these situations. Breaking tasks into smaller, more manageable steps, creating to-do lists, and setting realistic goals can help reduce the feeling of being overwhelmed and promote a sense of control.

5. Physical Exercise and Healthy Lifestyle:

Engaging in regular physical exercise has been shown to have a positive impact on anxiety levels. Exercise helps release endorphins, which improve mood and reduce stress. Additionally, adopting a healthy lifestyle by maintaining a balanced diet, getting sufficient sleep, and reducing the consumption of stimulants such as caffeine and alcohol can contribute to overall well-being and anxiety management.

6. **Social Support and Connection:**

Isolation can worsen anxiety symptoms, so building a support network and fostering social connections is crucial. Surrounding ourselves with understanding and supportive individuals provides a sense of belonging and validation. Sharing our concerns and experiences with trusted friends or family members can help alleviate anxiety and provide valuable perspective and support.

7. **Self-Care and Stress Reduction:**

Practicing self-care is essential for managing anxiety. Engaging in activities that bring joy, relaxation, and self-expression can help reduce stress levels. This may include hobbies, creative outlets, spending time in nature, or engaging in mindfulness practices. Engaging in stress-reducing activities nurtures our well-being and provides a respite from anxiety.

8. **Seeking Professional Help:**

If anxiety persists and significantly impacts daily life, seeking professional help is important. Mental health professionals, such as therapists or counselors, can provide guidance, support, and evidence-based interventions. They can tailor treatment plans specific to individual needs and utilize approaches like CBT, exposure therapy, or medication if necessary.

9. **Embracing Uncertainty and Resilience:**

Anxiety often stems from the need for control and certainty. Learning to embrace uncertainty and develop resilience in the face of life's challenges can reduce anxiety levels. Accepting that uncertainty is a natural part of life and that we have the strength to navigate through difficult situations builds our resilience. Cultivating a growth mindset, focusing on our strengths, and practicing self-compassion can help us approach uncertainties with greater ease and flexibility.

10. **Maintaining a Positive Lifestyle:**

Engaging in activities that promote positive emotions and well-being can have a profound impact on anxiety management. This includes spending time with loved ones, practicing gratitude, engaging in hobbies or interests, and finding moments of joy and laughter. Nurturing a positive mindset and incorporating activities that bring positivity into our lives can counterbalance the grip of anxiety.

11. **Seeking Balance:**

Anxiety often thrives in the extremes of our lives. Striving for balance in various areas, such as work, relationships, self-care, and leisure, can help manage anxiety. Setting boundaries, practicing self-compassion, and prioritizing self-care can prevent the accumulation of stress and maintain a sense of equilibrium.

12. **Continuous Learning and Growth:**

Managing anxiety is an ongoing journey that requires continuous learning and growth. Being open to new strategies, techniques, and self-reflection allows us to refine our coping skills and discover what works best for us individually. Seeking knowledge about anxiety, attending support groups, or participating in workshops can provide valuable insights and tools for managing anxiety effectively.

Taming the worry monster and managing anxiety is possible through a combination of strategies and a commitment to self-care and growth. By understanding anxiety, adopting relaxation techniques, challenging negative thoughts, practicing self-care, seeking support, and embracing resilience, we can gradually regain control over our lives and reduce the impact of anxiety. It is essential to remember that managing anxiety is a personal journey, and each individual may find certain strategies more effective than others. With patience, perseverance, and a proactive approach, we can tame the worry monster and cultivate a life marked by greater calm, well-being, and resilience.

Part III:
Illuminating Depression

Depression, often referred to as the silent struggle, is a complex and multifaceted mental health condition that affects millions of people worldwide. It casts a shadow over our thoughts, emotions, and overall well-being, making it difficult to navigate through the daily challenges of life. However, it is important to remember that there is light at the end of the tunnel, and by shedding light on depression, we can bring forth hope, understanding, and effective strategies for managing and overcoming this often debilitating condition.

In this third part of our journey, we aim to illuminate the depths of depression, unravel its intricacies, and offer guidance and support to those who may be experiencing its grip. We will delve into the nature of depression, explore its causes and symptoms, and highlight the various treatment options available. But most importantly, we will emphasize the transformative power of hope, resilience, and self-compassion in the face of depression.

1. **Understanding Depression:**

Depression is far more than just feeling sad or down. It is a mental health disorder characterized by a persistent feeling of sadness, hopelessness, and a loss of interest or pleasure in activities once enjoyed. It affects our thoughts, emotions, behaviors, and physical well-being, often leading to a sense of isolation and despair. By gaining a deeper understanding of depression, we can recognize its nuances, remove the stigma surrounding it, and foster an environment of empathy and support.

2. **Unveiling the Causes and Risk Factors:**

Depression is a complex condition with various contributing factors. It can be caused by a combination of genetic, biological, environmental, and psychological factors. Traumatic life events, chronic stress, a family history of depression, certain medical conditions, and imbalances in brain chemistry can all play a role in the development of depression. By exploring these causes and risk factors, we can better comprehend the unique experiences of individuals and tailor appropriate interventions.

3. **Recognizing the Symptoms:**

Depression manifests itself differently in each individual, but there are common symptoms that may indicate its presence. These can include persistent feelings of sadness or emptiness, changes in appetite or weight, sleep disturbances, loss of energy, difficulty concentrating, feelings of guilt or worthlessness, and thoughts of self-harm or suicide. It is crucial to be aware of these symptoms and seek help when they persist or significantly impact daily functioning.

4. **Treatment Options:**

The good news is that depression is treatable, and there are various options available for managing and overcoming it. Treatment plans often involve a combination of psychotherapy, medication, lifestyle changes, and self-care practices. Psychotherapy, such as cognitive-behavioral therapy (CBT) or interpersonal therapy, provides a safe and supportive space to explore underlying issues, challenge negative thought patterns, and develop effective coping strategies. Medications, such as antidepressants, can help correct chemical imbalances in the brain and alleviate depressive symptoms. Additionally, lifestyle changes, including regular exercise, healthy eating, sufficient sleep, and stress management, can have a significant positive impact on overall well-being.

5. **Building a Support Network:**

One of the most crucial aspects of navigating depression is the presence of a supportive network. Surrounding oneself with understanding and compassionate individuals who offer a listening ear, encouragement, and validation is invaluable. Friends, family members, support groups, or mental health professionals can provide a sense of belonging, reduce feelings of isolation, and offer guidance throughout the journey of healing.

6. **Cultivating Hope and Resilience:**

While depression may feel overwhelming and endless, it is essential to cultivate hope and resilience. Recognizing that depression does not define an individual's worth or future is crucial. By nurturing a positive mindset, setting realistic goals, celebrating small victories, and embracing self-compassion, individuals can tap into their inner strength and resilience. It is important to remember that recovery from depression is possible, and with the right support, treatment, and self-care, individuals can regain control of their lives and find joy and fulfillment once again.

7. **Self-Care and Well-being:**

Self-care is not a luxury; it is a vital component of managing and overcoming depression. Engaging in activities that promote self-nurturing, relaxation, and self-expression is essential. This may include practicing mindfulness and meditation, engaging in hobbies and creative outlets, spending time in nature, prioritizing rest and relaxation, and maintaining a healthy lifestyle. Taking care of one's physical, emotional, and mental well-being is a powerful tool in combating depression and fostering resilience.

8. **Seeking Help and Breaking the Silence:**

It is crucial to break the silence surrounding depression and reach out for help. Seeking professional assistance from mental health professionals, such as therapists, counselors, or psychiatrists, can provide the guidance and support needed on the journey toward recovery. These professionals have the knowledge and expertise to develop individualized treatment plans and provide evidence-based interventions. By seeking help, individuals can access the resources and tools necessary to navigate through the challenges of depression.

9. **Educating and Advocating:**

Education and advocacy play a vital role in destigmatizing depression and ensuring that individuals receive the support and understanding they deserve. By sharing personal stories, raising awareness, and promoting conversations about mental health, we can create a more compassionate and supportive society. Educating ourselves and others about depression helps break down barriers and encourages early intervention, ultimately saving lives and fostering a culture of empathy and acceptance.

10. **Embracing the Journey:**

Recovery from depression is not a linear path. It is important to embrace the ups and downs, setbacks, and small victories along the way. Each individual's journey is unique, and progress may take time. Patience, self-compassion, and self-acceptance are essential in navigating through the complexities of depression. By acknowledging that healing is a process, individuals can maintain hope and persevere even during challenging times.

In Part III of our exploration, we have embarked on a journey to illuminate depression, shed light on its causes, symptoms, and treatment options, and emphasize the transformative power of hope, resilience, and self-care. By understanding depression, seeking help, building a support network, and adopting self-care practices, individuals can navigate through the darkness and emerge into the light of recovery. Remember, you are not alone in this journey, and there is hope. With compassion, perseverance, and the right resources, it is possible to illuminate the path ahead and reclaim a life filled with purpose, joy, and well-being.

Understanding Depression: Types, Symptoms, and Diagnosis

Depression is a complex and pervasive mental health disorder that affects millions of people worldwide. It goes beyond the ordinary experience of sadness and encompasses a profound sense of despair, hopelessness, and emotional distress. Understanding the different types of depression, recognizing its symptoms, and obtaining an accurate diagnosis are crucial steps in addressing this debilitating condition. In this deep exploration, we will delve into the intricacies of depression, shedding light on its various forms, unraveling its symptoms, and discussing the importance of a comprehensive diagnosis.

Major Depressive Disorder:

Major Depressive Disorder (MDD), also known as clinical depression, is one of the most common forms of depression. It is characterized by persistent feelings of sadness, loss of interest or pleasure in activities, changes in appetite and sleep patterns, fatigue, difficulty concentrating, feelings of guilt or worthlessness, and recurrent thoughts of death or suicide. These symptoms typically last for at least two weeks and significantly impair an individual's daily functioning and overall quality of life.

Persistent Depressive Disorder:

Persistent Depressive Disorder (PDD), formerly known as dysthymia, is a chronic form of depression that lasts for two years or more. Individuals with PDD may experience milder symptoms compared to MDD, but they endure a persistent low mood, feelings of hopelessness, and a general lack of interest or pleasure in life. PDD can be challenging to diagnose as its symptoms may be less severe but persist for a more extended period, impacting long-term well-being.

Bipolar Disorder:

Bipolar Disorder is characterized by extreme mood swings that alternate between depressive episodes and manic or hypomanic episodes. During depressive episodes, individuals experience symptoms similar to those of MDD. However, during manic or hypomanic episodes, they may exhibit elevated moods, increased energy, impulsivity, racing thoughts, and reckless behavior. Bipolar Disorder requires careful assessment to distinguish between depressive and manic episodes to ensure an accurate diagnosis and appropriate treatment.

Postpartum Depression:

Postpartum Depression (PPD) is a type of depression that affects new mothers after childbirth. It is estimated that approximately 10-15% of women experience PPD, which is often characterized by intense feelings of sadness, exhaustion, irritability, guilt, and a loss of interest in the baby or inability to bond. PPD can significantly impact a mother's ability to care for herself and her child, emphasizing the importance of early detection and intervention.

Seasonal Affective Disorder:

Seasonal Affective Disorder (SAD) is a type of depression that occurs cyclically, typically during the fall and winter months when there is less natural sunlight. Individuals with SAD may experience symptoms such as fatigue, increased sleep, weight gain, irritability, and a decreased interest in activities. The limited exposure to sunlight disrupts the body's internal clock and can affect serotonin levels, contributing to depressive symptoms.

Symptoms of Depression:

Depressive symptoms can manifest in a variety of ways, and their severity and duration can vary from person to person. Common symptoms include persistent feelings of sadness, hopelessness, or emptiness, loss of interest or pleasure in activities, changes in appetite or weight, sleep disturbances, fatigue or loss of energy, difficulty concentrating or making decisions, feelings of guilt or worthlessness, and recurrent thoughts of death or suicide. It is essential to recognize these symptoms and seek professional help if they persist or significantly impact daily functioning.

Diagnosis and Seeking Professional Help:

Diagnosing depression requires a comprehensive evaluation by a qualified mental health professional. They will conduct a thorough assessment, including a detailed discussion of symptoms, medical history, and family history. The Diagnostic and Statistical Manual of Mental Disorders (DSM-5) provides a set of criteria used by mental health professionals to diagnose depression. It is crucial to seek professional help from a psychiatrist, psychologist, or licensed therapist who specializes in mental health to ensure an accurate diagnosis and appropriate treatment plan.

During the diagnostic process, the mental health professional may also conduct additional assessments or screenings to rule out other medical conditions or factors that could be contributing to the symptoms. This may involve blood tests, physical examinations, or consultations with other healthcare providers. A comprehensive diagnosis is essential as it guides the treatment approach and helps individuals better understand their condition.

It is important to remember that seeking help for depression is not a sign of weakness, but rather a courageous step towards healing and recovery. Mental health professionals are trained to provide support, guidance, and evidence-based treatments to individuals experiencing depression. They can offer a safe space to discuss thoughts, emotions, and experiences, and work collaboratively to develop a personalized treatment plan.

Treatment options for depression may include psychotherapy, medication, or a combination of both. Cognitive-behavioral therapy (CBT), interpersonal therapy (IPT), and psychodynamic therapy are among the therapeutic approaches commonly used to address the underlying causes of depression, challenge negative thought patterns, and develop coping strategies.

In some cases, medication, such as antidepressants, may be prescribed to help regulate brain chemistry and alleviate depressive symptoms. It is important to work closely with a healthcare provider to find the most suitable medication and dosage, as well as to monitor any potential side effects.

Additionally, lifestyle modifications can play a significant role in managing depression. Engaging in regular physical exercise, maintaining a balanced diet, practicing stress management techniques (such as mindfulness or relaxation exercises), ensuring adequate sleep, and fostering social connections can all contribute to improved mental well-being.

Support from loved ones, friends, or support groups can also provide invaluable encouragement and understanding throughout the journey of depression. Sharing experiences, seeking advice, and connecting with others who have similar experiences can help reduce feelings of isolation and provide a sense of belonging.

In conclusion, understanding the different types of depression, recognizing the symptoms, and obtaining an accurate diagnosis are crucial steps in addressing this challenging mental health condition. By seeking professional help, individuals can access appropriate treatment, support, and resources to navigate their journey towards healing and recovery. Remember, you are not alone, and there is hope for a brighter tomorrow. With proper support and effective interventions, it is possible to regain control, find solace, and embrace a life marked by resilience and well-being.

Navigating the Dark Days: Coping with Depression

Depression can cast a long and heavy shadow over our lives, engulfing us in a seemingly never-ending cycle of darkness, despair, and emotional pain. It can feel like an uphill battle, where even the simplest tasks become monumental challenges. Coping with depression requires courage, resilience, and a compassionate approach towards oneself. In this profound exploration, we will delve into the depths of depression, offering insights, strategies, and a sense of hope to those navigating the dark days.

1. Embracing Self-Compassion:

When faced with depression, it is vital to cultivate a sense of self-compassion. Depression often brings with it a barrage of negative thoughts, self-criticism, and feelings of worthlessness. It is crucial to remember that depression is an illness, not a personal failing. Treat yourself with kindness, understanding, and acceptance. Embrace self-care practices that nourish your mind, body, and soul. Engage in activities that bring you joy, practice mindfulness, and surround yourself with a support network that uplifts and encourages you.

2. Seeking Professional Help:

While self-care practices can be beneficial, it is essential to seek professional help when coping with depression. Mental health professionals, such as therapists, counselors, or psychiatrists, have the expertise to provide guidance, support, and evidence-based interventions. They can help you navigate the complexities of depression, offer coping strategies, and tailor treatment plans to your unique needs. Remember, reaching out for help is a sign of strength, not weakness.

3. **Building a Support Network:**

Surrounding yourself with a compassionate and understanding support network can make a significant difference in your journey with depression. Share your struggles with trusted friends, family members, or support groups who can provide a listening ear, empathy, and encouragement. Connecting with others who have experienced or are currently facing depression can foster a sense of camaraderie and remind you that you are not alone in your struggles.

4. **Engaging in Therapy:**

Therapy can be a valuable tool for coping with depression. Various therapeutic approaches, such as cognitive-behavioral therapy (CBT), dialectical behavior therapy (DBT), or psychodynamic therapy, can help you uncover underlying causes, challenge negative thought patterns, and develop effective coping strategies. Therapy provides a safe and non-judgmental space to explore your emotions, gain insights, and learn practical skills to manage and navigate the challenges of depression.

5. **Developing Coping Strategies:**

In addition to professional help, developing personal coping strategies is crucial when facing depression. Experiment with different techniques to find what works best for you. This may include engaging in regular exercise, which has been shown to boost mood and release endorphins. Exploring creative outlets such as art, music, or writing can provide a channel for self-expression and emotional release. Practicing relaxation techniques such as deep breathing, meditation, or yoga can help calm the mind and reduce anxiety.

6. Establishing Routine and Structure:

Depression often disrupts daily routines and leaves individuals feeling overwhelmed and unmotivated. Establishing a structured routine can provide a sense of stability and purpose. Set realistic goals and break them down into smaller, manageable tasks. Create a schedule that includes self-care activities, exercise, social interactions, and responsibilities. Having a routine can provide a sense of control, boost productivity, and contribute to a more positive outlook.

7. Taking Care of Physical Health:

Taking care of your physical health is integral to coping with depression. Ensure you are getting sufficient sleep, as sleep disturbances are common in depression. Practice good nutrition by consuming a balanced diet that includes fruits, vegetables, whole grains, and lean proteins. Limit the intake of alcohol and drugs, as they can exacerbate depressive symptoms.

8. Exploring Mindfulness and Relaxation:

Incorporating mindfulness and relaxation practices into your daily routine can be transformative when coping with depression. Mindfulness involves bringing your attention to the present moment without judgment, allowing you to observe your thoughts and emotions with greater clarity. Engaging in activities such as meditation, deep breathing exercises, or guided imagery can help reduce stress, promote emotional balance, and cultivate a sense of inner peace. These practices encourage self-awareness, self-compassion, and a gentle detachment from negative thought patterns.

9. Managing Stress:

Stress can exacerbate depressive symptoms and make it challenging to cope with depression effectively. Developing stress management techniques is crucial for maintaining emotional well-being. Identify stress triggers and find healthy ways to manage them. This may involve setting boundaries, practicing assertiveness, prioritizing self-care, and engaging in activities that promote relaxation and rejuvenation. Remember to pace yourself, be mindful of your limitations, and seek support when needed.

10. Finding Meaning and Purpose:

Depression can often leave individuals feeling lost and disconnected from a sense of meaning and purpose in life. Engage in activities that bring you a sense of fulfillment and joy. Explore your interests, set meaningful goals, and find ways to contribute to something greater than yourself. This might involve volunteering, pursuing hobbies, or engaging in creative endeavors. Connecting with your values and engaging in activities aligned with them can provide a renewed sense of purpose and direction.

11. Practicing Patience and Persistence:

Coping with depression is a journey that requires patience and persistence. Recovery may not happen overnight, and setbacks are normal. Be gentle with yourself during the process and celebrate even the smallest victories. Remind yourself that healing takes time, and progress may come in waves. Surround yourself with positive affirmations and reminders of your inner strength and resilience. Stay committed to self-care, therapy, and healthy coping strategies, even when it feels challenging.

12. **Embracing Hope:**

Above all, hold onto hope. Depression can make it difficult to envision a brighter future, but it is crucial to remind yourself that healing is possible. Surround yourself with stories of resilience and individuals who have overcome similar challenges. Engage in activities that inspire and uplift you. Cultivate a sense of gratitude for the small moments of joy and progress. Allow yourself to believe that there is a light at the end of the tunnel, even if it seems distant. Hope can be a guiding force that sustains you through the darkest days.

Coping with depression requires strength, resilience, and a multifaceted approach. By embracing self-compassion, seeking professional help, building a support network, developing coping strategies, establishing routines, taking care of physical health, exploring mindfulness, managing stress, finding meaning and purpose, practicing patience, and embracing hope, individuals can navigate the dark days and work towards a brighter future. Remember, you are not alone in this journey, and there are resources, support, and strategies available to help you along the way. Hold onto hope, believe in your ability to heal, and take each step forward with courage and determination.

Tools for Hope: Overcoming Depressive Thoughts and Behaviors

When facing the depths of depression, it can feel as if hope is a distant, elusive concept. The weight of depressive thoughts and behaviors can be suffocating, making it challenging to see a way out. However, within the darkness, there are tools that can ignite the flame of hope and empower individuals to overcome the grip of depression. In this profound exploration, we will delve into the transformative tools that can help navigate the path towards healing, resilience, and a brighter future.

1. **Cognitive Restructuring:**

Cognitive restructuring is a powerful tool for challenging and reframing negative thought patterns that contribute to depressive thinking. It involves recognizing and questioning the validity of negative beliefs, replacing them with more realistic and positive thoughts. By examining evidence and considering alternative perspectives, individuals can gradually shift their mindset from self-criticism and hopelessness to self-compassion and optimism. Working with a therapist or utilizing self-help resources can provide guidance and support in mastering this tool.

2. **Behavioral Activation:**

Depression often leads to a withdrawal from activities and a loss of interest in things once enjoyed. Behavioral activation focuses on breaking this cycle by engaging in positive and meaningful activities, even when motivation is low. By scheduling and participating in activities that align with personal values and interests, individuals can experience a sense of accomplishment, pleasure, and purpose. Gradually increasing the level of engagement and incorporating social connections can further enhance the benefits of behavioral activation.

3. **Mindfulness and Meditation:**

Practicing mindfulness and meditation can be transformative in managing depressive thoughts and behaviors. Mindfulness involves non-judgmental awareness of the present moment, allowing individuals to observe their thoughts and emotions without getting caught up in them. It cultivates a sense of acceptance, self-compassion, and emotional regulation. Regular meditation practice can help quiet the mind, reduce stress, and foster a deeper connection with oneself. Guided meditation apps, mindfulness courses, or working with a mindfulness coach can provide guidance and structure.

4. **Gratitude Practice:**

Cultivating a gratitude practice can shift the focus from negativity to appreciation, fostering a sense of hope and contentment. Each day, intentionally identify and acknowledge things, big or small, that you are grateful for. This could include moments of joy, supportive relationships, personal strengths, or acts of kindness. Engaging in this practice rewires the brain to notice and savor positive experiences, gradually reshaping the overall perspective towards a more hopeful and optimistic outlook.

5. **Journaling:**

Writing can be a powerful tool for exploring and processing emotions, gaining insights, and challenging negative thought patterns. Consider keeping a journal where you can freely express your thoughts, feelings, and experiences. Use it as a space for self-reflection, gratitude, setting goals, or recording positive moments. Journaling can provide a sense of release, clarity, and self-discovery, serving as a tangible reminder of progress, resilience, and personal growth.

6. **Social Support:**

Building a strong social support network is vital in overcoming depressive thoughts and behaviors. Reach out to trusted friends, family members, or support groups who can offer understanding, empathy, and encouragement. Share your experiences, seek advice, and lean on their support during difficult times. Engaging in meaningful connections and open communication can alleviate feelings of isolation and provide a sense of belonging, fostering hope and resilience.

7. **Self-Care:**

Prioritizing self-care is essential when overcoming depression. Engage in activities that nourish your physical, emotional, and mental well-being. This could include getting enough sleep, practicing good nutrition, engaging in regular exercise, and engaging in activities that bring joy and relaxation. Remember to set boundaries, practice self-compassion, and make self-care a non-negotiable part of your daily

8. **Professional Support:**

Seeking professional support is crucial when navigating depressive thoughts and behaviors. Mental health professionals, such as therapists, counselors, or psychiatrists, can offer specialized guidance, evidence-based interventions, and a safe space for exploration and healing. They can help identify underlying causes, develop personalized treatment plans, and provide ongoing support throughout the recovery journey.

In the face of depressive thoughts and behaviors, tools for hope are essential. By employing cognitive restructuring, behavioral activation, mindfulness, gratitude practice, journaling, social support, self-care, and professional help, individuals can regain control, challenge negative patterns, and cultivate resilience. These tools provide the strength and guidance to navigate the darkest moments, transform the perception of self and the world, and reclaim a life filled with hope, purpose, and well-being. Remember, within you lies the power to overcome, to heal, and to embrace a future illuminated by possibilities.

In exploring the tools for overcoming depressive thoughts and behaviors, it is enlightening to delve into the perspectives of renowned psychologists who have made significant contributions to the field of mental health. Their insights offer valuable guidance and inspiration in the journey towards healing and resilience.

1. **Cognitive Restructuring - Inspired by Aaron Beck:**

The tool of cognitive restructuring finds its roots in the cognitive therapy developed by Aaron Beck. Beck emphasized the importance of identifying and challenging negative automatic thoughts that contribute to depressive thinking. Drawing on Beck's work, individuals can actively examine the evidence supporting their negative beliefs, reframe distorted thinking patterns, and cultivate more balanced and realistic perspectives. By recognizing the power of our thoughts and actively reshaping them, we can create a cognitive shift that leads to greater hope and well-being.

2. **Behavioral Activation - Influenced by Martin Seligman:**

Martin Seligman, a pioneer in positive psychology, has highlighted the significance of behavioral activation in overcoming depression. Seligman's work emphasizes the importance of engaging in activities that bring a sense of pleasure, mastery, and meaning. By following Seligman's principles, individuals can identify and pursue activities aligned with their values and strengths, fostering a sense of accomplishment and fulfillment. This approach encourages individuals to break free from the cycle of withdrawal and gradually reintroduce joy and purpose into their lives.

3. **Mindfulness and Meditation - Guided by Jon Kabat-Zinn:**

The practice of mindfulness and meditation has been popularized by Jon Kabat-Zinn, who developed the Mindfulness-Based Stress Reduction (MBSR) program. Kabat-Zinn's teachings emphasize the power of present-moment awareness, acceptance, and non-judgment. By incorporating mindfulness into daily life, individuals can observe their thoughts and emotions without getting entangled in them, cultivating a sense of inner peace and resilience. Kabat-Zinn's approach encourages individuals to embrace mindfulness as a tool for reducing suffering, managing stress, and fostering a positive mental outlook.

4. **Gratitude Practice - Inspired by Robert Emmons:**

Robert Emmons, a leading researcher in the field of positive psychology, has extensively studied the effects of gratitude on well-being. Emmons emphasizes the transformative power of cultivating a gratitude practice. By acknowledging and appreciating the positive aspects of life, individuals can shift their focus from what is lacking to what is present, fostering a sense of hope, contentment, and resilience. Emmons' work encourages individuals to integrate gratitude into their daily lives, recognizing its potential to counteract depressive thoughts and enhance overall well-being.

5. **Social Support - Influenced by Irvin Yalom:**

Irvin Yalom, a prominent existential psychotherapist, has emphasized the significance of social connections in the process of healing and self-discovery. Yalom's work highlights the healing power of interpersonal relationships, as they provide a sense of belonging, empathy, and validation. Drawing from Yalom's perspective, individuals can seek out supportive relationships, join therapeutic groups, or engage in community activities that foster connection and understanding. By surrounding themselves with a supportive network, individuals can gain strength, resilience, and hope in their journey towards overcoming depression.

In conclusion, by embracing the tools for hope rooted in the wisdom of psychologists like Aaron Beck, Martin Seligman, Jon Kabat-Zinn, Robert Emmons, and Irvin Yalom, individuals can navigate their way out of the depths of depression. By actively engaging in cognitive restructuring, behavioral activation, mindfulness and meditation, gratitude practice, and social support, individuals can reclaim their lives, transform their perspectives, and cultivate resilience. These diverse tools offer a multi-faceted approach to healing and empower individuals to overcome depressive thoughts and behaviors, ultimately guiding them towards a future characterized by hope, well-being, and personal growth.

Once Upon a time,

in the tranquil embrace of a cozy cottage nestled amidst a sprawling meadow, where wildflowers swayed in the gentle breeze and the chorus of birds filled the air, there lived a young soul named Emily. Within the walls that held her hopes and fears, Emily navigated the treacherous terrain of depression, a journey that would test her resilience and ultimately guide her towards the light of healing.

Emily's story unfolded in a world that often concealed the harsh realities of mental health struggles behind masks of pretense and societal expectations. As she ventured through the labyrinth of her daily existence, Emily fought a silent battle with the relentless grip of depression. Days stretched into nights, and a heavy fog obscured her path, making it difficult to see beyond the shadows that enveloped her spirit.

One fateful day, as raindrops danced upon the windowpane, Emily stumbled upon a weathered journal tucked away in the dusty attic of her cottage. Its leather cover bore the words "Navigating the Dark Days: Coping with Depression," a profound guide written by a renowned psychologist, Dr. Alexander Bennett. Intrigued by the promise of guidance and understanding, Emily opened the journal, eager to discover the wisdom held within its pages.

With each carefully crafted sentence, Dr. Bennett's words resonated deeply within Emily's weary heart. She found solace in the shared stories of others who had traversed the labyrinth of darkness, emerging with newfound strength and resilience. The journal became a cherished companion, a sanctuary where Emily could pour out her deepest fears, thoughts, and emotions without judgment or fear of rejection.

Within the journal's intimate confines, Emily unearthed a plethora of coping strategies and tools, carefully curated by Dr. Bennett's expertise. She learned the art of self-care, cultivating rituals that nourished her mind, body, and spirit. From soothing baths infused with lavender to meditative walks in nature's embrace, Emily discovered the transformative power of tending to her own well-being.

Embracing the concept of self-compassion, Emily gently untangled the knots of self-criticism that had entwined her spirit for far too long. Dr. Bennett's words guided her towards acceptance and understanding, allowing her to view her journey through a lens of empathy and kindness. She learned to grant herself grace on the darkest days, understanding that healing was a nonlinear path, with setbacks and triumphs woven intricately together.
Driven by an insatiable thirst for knowledge and growth, Emily sought additional resources beyond the journal's pages. She delved into the works of renowned psychologists and mental health experts, immersing herself in the writings of luminaries such as Dr. Viktor Frankl, Dr. Brené Brown, and Dr. Elizabeth Blackburn. Their words became beacons of inspiration, guiding her towards profound insights and a deeper understanding of her own journey. Armed with newfound knowledge and resilience, Emily courageously reached out for professional support. With the guidance of a compassionate therapist, she embarked on a therapeutic voyage, unearthing the roots of her pain and addressing the wounds that had long been ignored. Through talk therapy, cognitive-behavioral techniques, and the power of human connection, Emily learned to reframe her negative thought patterns and cultivate a more positive and empowering mindset.
As time unfurled its tapestry, Emily's transformation became evident to those around her. Her spirit, once weighed down by the heavy burden of depression, began to radiate with a newfound vitality. She embraced her journey as a testament to the strength of

the human spirit and became an advocate for mental health, sharing her story with honesty and vulnerability, allowing others to see themselves reflected in her experiences.

Through the labyrinth of her own journey, Emily discovered that navigating the dark days of depression was not a solitary endeavor. She found solace in the support of loved ones, forging deeper connections and allowing vulnerability to pave the way for authentic relationships. In her darkest moments, she realized that she was never alone, and that reaching out for support was not a sign of weakness but an act of courage and self-preservation. Emily's story, a tapestry woven with resilience, self-discovery, and unwavering determination, serves as a beacon of hope for those who find themselves grappling with the shadows of depression. As she continues her journey, Emily embraces each new day with renewed purpose, knowing that even amidst the darkness, the light of healing and transformation can flicker and ignite, guiding others towards their own path of recovery and strength.

Part IV: Healing and Overcoming

The journey of healing and overcoming is a profound and transformative process that individuals embark upon when faced with adversity, be it depression, anxiety, or other mental health challenges. It is a path filled with resilience, self-discovery, and the pursuit of inner strength. Part IV delves into the depths of this journey, shedding light on the tools, strategies, and perspectives that can guide individuals towards healing and triumph. It is a testament to the human spirit, illustrating that even in the face of darkness, there is the potential for growth, empowerment, and a renewed sense of purpose.

1. **Embracing Self-Compassion:**

Healing and overcoming begin with the act of embracing self-compassion. It is the recognition that one's struggles do not define their worth or potential. Self-compassion invites individuals to treat themselves with kindness, understanding, and patience as they navigate the challenges on their path to healing. By extending compassion towards oneself, individuals can cultivate resilience, foster self-acceptance, and create a nurturing environment for personal growth.

2. **Cultivating Resilience:**

Resilience is the capacity to adapt, bounce back, and thrive in the face of adversity. It is a quality that lies within each individual and can be nurtured and strengthened. Cultivating resilience involves developing healthy coping mechanisms, building a support network, and reframing setbacks as opportunities for growth. By harnessing resilience, individuals can weather the storms, rise above obstacles, and find renewed strength on their journey towards healing.

3. **Unleashing the Power of Vulnerability:**

In vulnerability lies the potential for profound healing and transformation. Embracing vulnerability is an act of courage, as it requires individuals to acknowledge their pain, fears, and insecurities. By opening up, seeking support, and sharing their experiences, individuals create spaces for authentic connections, empathy, and understanding. It is through vulnerability that healing can take root, allowing individuals to release the weight of their burdens and find solace in the collective human experience.

4. **Seeking Professional Guidance:**

While personal strength and self-discovery are essential, seeking professional guidance is a vital step on the path to healing and overcoming. Mental health professionals, such as therapists, counselors, or psychiatrists, possess the expertise and tools to provide support, guidance, and evidence-based interventions. Their presence can offer validation, perspective, and a safe space for individuals to explore their emotions, past traumas, and deep-rooted patterns. With their assistance, individuals can navigate the complexities of their journey with professional insight and personalized strategies.

5. **Engaging in Holistic Self-Care:**

Healing and overcoming extend beyond addressing the mind; they encompass holistic self-care. Nurturing the body, mind, and spirit is paramount for well-being and resilience. Engaging in activities that promote physical health, such as regular exercise, balanced nutrition, and sufficient rest, creates a solid foundation for healing. Equally important is tending to emotional well-being through self-reflection, creativity, and engaging in activities that bring joy and fulfillment. Taking care of the spirit involves connecting with one's values, finding purpose, and fostering a sense of inner peace.

6. **Embracing Growth and Personal Transformation:**

Healing and overcoming are transformative processes that allow individuals to evolve, grow, and discover new dimensions of themselves. It requires embracing change, challenging limiting beliefs, and actively pursuing personal growth. Through self-reflection, introspection, and continuous learning, individuals can shed old patterns, develop new perspectives, and cultivate a sense of empowerment. Healing becomes a catalyst for personal transformation, unveiling strengths and capacities that were previously untapped.

7. **Sharing and Inspiring Others:**

As individuals progress on their healing journey, they have the power to inspire and support others who may be walking a similar path. By sharing their experiences, insights, and lessons learned, individuals can offer a guiding light to those who are still in the midst of their struggles. Through storytelling, advocacy, or participating in support groups, individuals can create a ripple effect of healing, compassion, and hope within their communities.

Part IV: Healing and Overcoming is an exploration of the profound journey individuals undertake when faced with mental health challenges. By embracing self-compassion, cultivating resilience, unleashing the power of vulnerability, seeking professional guidance, engaging in holistic self-care, embracing growth, and sharing their experiences, individuals can navigate the path towards healing and triumph. It is a testament to the indomitable human spirit, revealing the boundless potential for growth, resilience, and the emergence of a renewed sense of purpose and well-being. May this exploration serve as a beacon of hope, reminding us that healing is not only possible but a transformative and empowering process.

The Power of Self-Care: Nurturing Your Mind, Body, and Spirit

In the hustle and bustle of everyday life, it is easy to neglect our own well-being as we prioritize the demands and expectations placed upon us. However, the power of self-care cannot be underestimated. Nurturing our mind, body, and spirit is not a luxury but a necessity for maintaining balance, resilience, and overall well-being. In this exploration, we delve into the transformative power of self-care, recognizing its profound impact on our mental, physical, and emotional health. By prioritizing self-care, we empower ourselves to navigate life's challenges, cultivate inner strength, and embrace a life of greater fulfillment and harmony.

1. **Mind: Cultivating Mental Well-Being**

Nurturing our mind involves taking deliberate actions to cultivate mental well-being. This can include practicing mindfulness and meditation to quiet the mind, reduce stress, and enhance self-awareness. Engaging in activities that stimulate creativity, such as writing, painting, or playing an instrument, allows us to express ourselves and tap into our inner thoughts and emotions. Seeking knowledge through reading, learning, or engaging in stimulating conversations expands our perspective and fosters personal growth. Taking time for solitude and reflection provides an opportunity to recharge, gain clarity, and nourish our mental landscape.

2. **Body: Prioritizing Physical Health**

Caring for our bodies is an essential aspect of self-care. Prioritizing physical health involves engaging in regular exercise to promote cardiovascular fitness, strength, and flexibility. Whether it's walking, running, yoga, or dancing, finding activities that bring joy and movement to our bodies is crucial. Nourishing our bodies with a balanced and nutritious diet supports overall well-being and vitality. Sufficient rest and quality sleep rejuvenate our bodies and allow for optimal functioning. Taking care of our physical health not only improves our energy levels but also enhances our resilience and ability to navigate life's challenges.

3. **Spirit: Connecting with Inner Self**

Nurturing our spirit involves connecting with our inner self, our values, and our sense of purpose. Engaging in activities that bring joy and fulfillment, such as spending time in nature, practicing gratitude, or engaging in acts of kindness, nourishes our spirit. Exploring our passions, hobbies, or creative pursuits ignites our inner spark and cultivates a sense of meaning and purpose. Engaging in spiritual practices or rituals, such as prayer, meditation, or journaling, deepens our connection with something greater than ourselves and fosters a sense of inner peace and tranquility.

4. **Boundaries: Honoring Your Needs**

Setting and maintaining healthy boundaries is an integral part of self-care. It involves recognizing and honoring our needs, both physically and emotionally, and communicating them effectively to others. Establishing boundaries allows us to protect our time, energy, and emotional well-being. It empowers us to say no to activities or relationships that drain us and yes to those that nourish and support our growth. By asserting our boundaries, we create a space for self-care, self-respect, and personal empowerment.

5. **Self-Compassion: Cultivating Kindness**

Self-compassion is a vital component of self-care. It involves treating ourselves with kindness, understanding, and acceptance, especially in times of difficulty or setbacks. Practicing self-compassion allows us to acknowledge our imperfections and mistakes without judgment. It means being gentle with ourselves, practicing self-forgiveness, and embracing our humanness. By cultivating self-compassion, we create a nurturing inner environment that supports our well-being and encourages personal growth.

6. **Connection: Nurturing Relationships**

Human connection is a fundamental aspect of self-care. Nurturing relationships with loved ones, friends, and communities provides us with a sense of belonging, support, and emotional nourishment. Investing time and effort in fostering meaningful connections allows us to feel seen, heard, and valued. Engaging in acts of kindness, empathy, and active listening strengthens our relationships and cultivates a sense of fulfillment and purpose.

The power of self-care is transformative and profound. By nurturing our mind, body, and spirit, setting healthy boundaries, practicing self-compassion, and fostering connections, we create a foundation of well-being and resilience. It is through self-care that we replenish our energy, find balance amidst life's challenges, and unlock our true potential. As we prioritize self-care, we not only enhance our own well-being but also create a ripple effect, inspiring others to do the same. Embrace the power of self-care and embark on a journey of self-discovery, empowerment, and greater fulfillment in all aspects of your life. Remember, you deserve the love, care, and nurturing that self-care provides.

Here are some real-life examples of self-care practices that nurture the mind, body, and spirit:

Mind:

Practicing mindfulness meditation for a few minutes each day to cultivate present-moment awareness and reduce stress.

Engaging in journaling or expressive writing to reflect on thoughts, emotions, and experiences.

Reading books on personal development, psychology, or topics of interest to expand knowledge and stimulate the mind.

Body:

Engaging in regular physical exercise, such as going for a jog, attending a fitness class, or practicing yoga.

Prioritizing nutritious meals and incorporating wholesome foods into daily diet.

Getting enough sleep and establishing a consistent bedtime routine for quality rest and rejuvenation.

Spirit:

Spending time in nature, whether it's going for a hike, gardening, or simply sitting in a park to connect with the natural world.

Practicing gratitude by keeping a gratitude journal or sharing three things they are grateful for each day.

Engaging in a spiritual practice that aligns with personal beliefs, such as prayer, meditation, or attending religious services.

Boundaries:

Learning to say no to commitments or activities that do not align with personal values or drain energy.

Setting aside designated "me-time" for self-reflection, relaxation, or engaging in hobbies and interests.

Communicating needs and boundaries clearly and assertively with others.

Self-Compassion:

Engaging in positive self-talk and offering oneself words of encouragement and support during challenging times. Practicing self-forgiveness and letting go of self-judgment or regrets.

Engaging in self-care activities without guilt, acknowledging that self-care is essential for well-being.

Connection:

Nurturing relationships by scheduling quality time with loved ones, engaging in meaningful conversations, or planning activities together.

Participating in social or community activities that align with personal interests or values.

Seeking support from a therapist, counselor, or support group to foster connections with others who share similar experiences.

Remember, these examples are just a starting point, and it's essential to personalize self-care practices based on individual preferences and needs. Experiment with different activities and find what brings you joy, relaxation, and a sense of fulfillment.

Once Upon a time,

in a quiet suburban neighborhood, nestled amidst friendly neighbors and blooming gardens, there lived a teenager named Alex. Like many young individuals, Alex traversed the intricate maze of adolescence, facing their own unique set of challenges. Amidst the whispers of self-doubt and the shadows of anxiety and depression, Alex yearned for a way to break free and discover their own inner strength.

Within the serenity of their neighborhood, Alex found solace in nature's embrace. The rustling leaves whispered words of encouragement, and the vibrant flowers seemed to offer a gentle reminder that beauty can bloom even in the midst of adversity. It was in this tranquil setting that Alex's transformative journey began, with the support of a few special mentors who would play pivotal roles in their life.

One such mentor was Mrs. Jenkins, a wise and compassionate neighbor who had experienced her own battles with mental health. Recognizing the struggles that weighed heavily on Alex's young shoulders, she extended a caring hand and opened her heart to them. Through her gentle guidance and heartfelt conversations on her porch swing, Mrs. Jenkins shared her own stories of resilience and the power of self-discovery.

Another key figure in Alex's journey was their school counselor, Mr. Ramirez. With his warm smile and attentive ears, Mr. Ramirez created a safe haven within the school's bustling hallways. He patiently listened as Alex poured out their fears and worries, helping them navigate the maze of emotions and offering valuable insights and coping strategies. Together, they explored the depths *of Alex's thoughts and feelings, gradually unraveling the tangled threads of anxiety and depression.*

As the days turned into weeks and the weeks into months, Alex discovered a newfound resilience within themselves. They embarked on a path of self-care, exploring different practices that nurtured their mind, body, and spirit. Yoga and meditation became their daily companions, allowing them to cultivate inner peace and connect with their own inner wisdom.

Alex's journey of healing and empowerment extended beyond the confines of their neighborhood and school. They found solace in online communities, where they connected with fellow young individuals who shared similar struggles. Together, they formed a virtual support network, offering words of encouragement, sharing resources, and reminding one another that they were not alone in their battle.

Inspired by their own transformation, Alex began to advocate for mental health awareness within their school and community. They organized workshops, initiated conversations, and collaborated with local organizations to promote understanding and empathy. Through their passionate efforts, they became a beacon of hope for their peers, proving that healing and empowerment were within reach.

As time passed, Alex continued to thrive, not without setbacks and challenges, but armed with newfound resilience and an unwavering spirit. Their story of healing and empowerment resonated with young individuals far and wide, as they realized that within their own journeys lay the power to rewrite their narratives and find the light that guided them towards a life of fulfillment and purpose.

Alex's story serves as a reminder to all young souls navigating their own paths that healing and empowerment are not distant dreams but tangible realities. It is in the embrace of kind mentors, the discovery of self-care practices, and the strength found in community that they can emerge from the shadows of anxiety and depression, ready to embrace a future filled with endless possibilities.

Therapeutic Approaches: Seeking Professional Help and Treatment Options

In the intricate tapestry of human existence, there are moments when life becomes overwhelming, when the burdens we carry feel too heavy to bear alone. During such times, seeking professional help and exploring therapeutic approaches can be a beacon of hope, guiding us towards healing and transformation. By opening ourselves to the support and expertise of trained professionals, we gain access to a wealth of resources, tools, and strategies to navigate the challenges we face.

Therapeutic approaches encompass a vast array of techniques and modalities tailored to address various mental health concerns. These approaches are designed to foster insight, facilitate personal growth, and empower individuals to overcome their struggles. Whether one is grappling with anxiety, depression, trauma, or any other psychological difficulty, there exists a rich tapestry of therapeutic options to explore.

One widely recognized therapeutic approach is cognitive-behavioral therapy (CBT). Grounded in the belief that our thoughts, feelings, and behaviors are interconnected, CBT helps individuals identify and challenge negative or distorted thinking patterns. Through collaboration with a trained therapist, individuals learn to reframe their thoughts, develop healthier coping strategies, and ultimately transform their emotional and behavioral responses. CBT has demonstrated effectiveness in addressing a wide range of mental health issues, making it a versatile and widely utilized therapeutic approach.

Another approach gaining traction is dialectical behavior therapy (DBT). Originally developed to treat individuals with borderline personality disorder, DBT has since been adapted to address a variety of mental health challenges. DBT combines elements of mindfulness, distress tolerance, emotion regulation, and interpersonal effectiveness to help individuals build skills to manage intense emotions, develop healthy relationships, and cultivate a sense of balance and stability in their lives. Its holistic approach makes DBT particularly effective for those struggling with self-destructive behaviors, chronic suicidal thoughts, or difficulties in managing emotions.

For those who have experienced trauma, eye movement desensitization and reprocessing (EMDR) is a therapeutic approach that offers profound healing. EMDR harnesses the brain's innate capacity to process and heal from traumatic experiences. Through guided eye movements or other forms of bilateral stimulation, individuals engage in a structured process that allows traumatic memories to be reprocessed, resulting in a reduction of distressing symptoms. EMDR is often heralded as a transformative approach for those grappling with post-traumatic stress disorder (PTSD) or other trauma-related conditions.

In addition to these specific therapeutic approaches, there are various other modalities and techniques available. Psychodynamic therapy explores the unconscious aspects of the self, focusing on uncovering unresolved conflicts and deep-seated patterns of behavior. Acceptance and commitment therapy (ACT) emphasizes mindfulness and acceptance, guiding individuals to align their actions with their deeply held values. Art therapy, music therapy, and dance movement therapy provide creative outlets for expression and exploration of emotions. These are just a few examples of the diverse therapeutic landscape that exists, with each approach offering its own unique set of tools and benefits.

It is important to note that seeking professional help does not imply weakness or failure but rather demonstrates courage and a commitment to self-care. Engaging in therapy is an act of self-compassion, an acknowledgment that we deserve support and guidance during difficult times. Therapists provide a safe and non-judgmental space, offering empathy, expertise, and a listening ear. They work collaboratively with individuals to identify goals, develop personalized treatment plans, and provide evidence-based interventions that can facilitate healing and growth.

Beyond the therapeutic approaches mentioned, there are also various treatment options to consider. Medication can play a valuable role in managing certain mental health conditions, and psychiatrists are specialized medical professionals who can prescribe and monitor medications. Group therapy provides an opportunity to connect with others who share similar struggles, offering a sense of community and shared understanding. Support groups, community resources, and online platforms further extend the support network available to individuals seeking professional help.

It is crucial to remember that therapy is not a linear process, nor does it offer quick-fix solutions. Healing takes time, patience, and commitment. The therapeutic journey may involve setbacks, moments of vulnerability, and deep introspection. However, within this process lies the potential for profound growth, self-discovery, and lasting change.

As we embark on the path of seeking professional help and exploring therapeutic approaches, let us embrace the opportunity to nurture our mental well-being. Let us approach this journey with open hearts and open minds, knowing that we possess the strength to overcome our challenges. Together with the support of skilled professionals, we can navigate the labyrinth of our inner worlds, unraveling the knots that bind us and moving toward a life of greater authenticity, resilience, and fulfillment.

Here are a few examples of renowned psychologists who have made significant contributions to the field of therapy and have supported the importance of seeking professional help and treatment options:

1.Dr. Carl Rogers: Known for his person-centered approach to therapy, Carl Rogers emphasized the significance of creating a safe and supportive therapeutic environment. He believed in the inherent potential for growth and self-actualization within individuals and advocated for the therapeutic relationship as a catalyst for personal transformation.

2.Dr. Aaron Beck: As the founder of cognitive therapy, Aaron Beck has played a pivotal role in shaping the field of psychotherapy. His work focused on identifying and challenging distorted thinking patterns that contribute to psychological distress. Beck's research and techniques have been instrumental in the development of cognitive-behavioral therapy (CBT) and its widespread application in treating various mental health conditions.

3.Dr. Marsha M. Linehan: Marsha Linehan is the creator of dialectical behavior therapy (DBT), which combines elements of cognitive-behavioral therapy with mindfulness and acceptance-based strategies. Her work has been particularly influential in helping individuals with borderline personality disorder, self-harm behaviors, and difficulties regulating emotions.

4.Dr. Francine Shapiro: Known for her development of eye movement desensitization and reprocessing (EMDR), Francine Shapiro has revolutionized trauma therapy. EMDR has become widely recognized as an effective treatment for PTSD and has garnered empirical support for its ability to help individuals process and heal from traumatic experiences.

5.Dr. Irvin Yalom: Irvin Yalom is renowned for his work in existential psychotherapy. He explores themes such as meaning, mortality, and personal responsibility within the therapeutic context. Yalom's emphasis on the therapeutic relationship, existential concerns, and the search for meaning has resonated with many individuals seeking therapy.

These psychologists and their groundbreaking contributions highlight the transformative potential of seeking professional help and treatment options. Their work has not only shaped the field of psychology but also influenced the lives of countless individuals who have benefited from therapeutic interventions. By drawing upon their expertise and research, we gain insight into the profound impact that therapy can have on our well-being and personal growth.

It's important to note that this list is not exhaustive, and there are numerous other psychologists who have made significant contributions to the field of therapy. Exploring their research, writings, and approaches can provide further inspiration and understanding of the value of seeking professional help and treatment options.

Building Resilience: Strategies for Long-Term Recovery

In the face of life's challenges, building resilience becomes an invaluable asset–a cornerstone of our ability to navigate adversity, recover from setbacks, and cultivate long-term well-being. Resilience is not a fixed trait; rather, it is a dynamic quality that can be developed and nurtured over time. It empowers us to bounce back from adversity, adapt to change, and find meaning and growth in the face of adversity.

Building resilience requires a multifaceted approach that encompasses various strategies and practices. These strategies act as anchors, providing stability and support as we weather life's storms. By incorporating them into our daily lives, we can cultivate a foundation of strength and resourcefulness that allows us to thrive even in the most challenging circumstances.

One fundamental aspect of building resilience is fostering a positive mindset. Cultivating optimism, gratitude, and self-compassion can help reframe our experiences and build a sense of hope and resilience. Embracing a growth mindset–a belief that challenges are opportunities for growth and learning –enables us to approach setbacks with curiosity and resilience, rather than succumbing to defeat. By focusing on our strengths and accomplishments, we can cultivate a positive self-image that bolsters our resilience in the face of adversity.

Nurturing social connections is another critical element in building resilience. Cultivating supportive relationships and fostering a sense of belonging create a strong support network that can uplift us during difficult times. Sharing our challenges, seeking guidance, and offering support to others fosters a sense of mutual understanding and camaraderie. It is through these connections that we find solace, encouragement, and the reminder that we are not alone in our struggles.

Additionally, developing effective coping mechanisms is essential for building resilience. Engaging in activities that promote self-care and stress reduction, such as exercise, meditation, or engaging in hobbies, can help regulate our emotions and promote a sense of calm and well-being. Building a toolkit of healthy coping strategies equips us with the resources needed to navigate stress and adversity effectively.

Furthermore, cultivating adaptability and flexibility is crucial for long-term recovery. Life is unpredictable, and the ability to adapt to change and embrace new possibilities is an essential aspect of resilience. By embracing a mindset of flexibility and openness, we can navigate unexpected challenges with greater ease and resilience.

Psychologists and researchers have also identified the power of finding meaning and purpose as a key component of resilience. Discovering and aligning ourselves with our core values and goals provides a sense of direction and resilience in the face of adversity. When we can connect our experiences to a larger sense of purpose or find meaning in the lessons learned from challenges, we develop a profound resilience that propels us forward.

Additionally, it is important to seek professional help when needed. Mental health professionals can provide guidance, support, and evidence-based interventions tailored to individual needs. Therapy can help individuals develop coping strategies, process difficult emotions, and gain valuable insights that promote long-term recovery and resilience.

Drawing inspiration from the wisdom of psychologists such as Martin Seligman, who pioneered the field of positive psychology, and Viktor Frankl, who emphasized the power of finding meaning in life's challenges, we can deepen our understanding of resilience and its transformative potential. Their research and writings provide valuable insights and practical strategies for cultivating resilience and achieving long-term recovery.

In conclusion, building resilience is a dynamic and ongoing journey that requires intention, practice, and self-reflection. By nurturing a positive mindset, fostering social connections, developing effective coping mechanisms, cultivating adaptability, finding meaning and purpose, and seeking professional help when needed, we can strengthen our resilience and foster long-term recovery. With resilience as our guiding light, we can navigate life's trials with courage, grace, and a steadfast belief in our ability to overcome and thrive.

The following examples and references provide a glimpse into the wealth of research and insights available on building resilience and strategies for long-term recovery.

Example: Olympic athletes often face intense challenges and setbacks throughout their careers. Their ability to bounce back and maintain a high level of performance is a testament to their resilience. Many athletes, such as Michael Phelps and Simone Biles, have openly discussed their struggles with mental health and how they have utilized strategies like therapy, mindfulness, and support networks to build resilience and continue their athletic journeys.

Reference: The American Psychological Association (APA) has extensive resources on building resilience. Their website provides information, articles, and practical tips on developing resilience in various contexts, including personal life, work, and community. The APA's "Road to Resilience" guide offers valuable insights and strategies for building resilience in the face of adversity.

Example: Dr. Angela Duckworth, a psychologist and researcher, is well-known for her work on the concept of "grit" and its relationship to resilience. She emphasizes the importance of perseverance, passion, and long-term goals in building resilience and achieving success. Her book "Grit: The Power of Passion and Perseverance" explores the science of resilience and provides practical guidance for cultivating resilience in various domains of life.

Reference: Dr. Martin Seligman, often considered the father of positive psychology, has conducted extensive research on resilience and well-being. His work emphasizes the role of positive emotions, character strengths, and finding meaning and purpose in promoting resilience. His books, including "Authentic Happiness" and "Flourish," delve into the science of well-being and offer insights into building resilience.

Example: The concept of post-traumatic growth highlights the potential for personal growth and resilience following traumatic experiences. Psychologists like Dr. Richard Tedeschi and Dr. Lawrence Calhoun have extensively researched this phenomenon, exploring how individuals can find new meaning, personal strength, and a renewed sense of purpose after going through challenging circumstances.

Reference: The book "Option B: Facing Adversity, Building Resilience, and Finding Joy" by Sheryl Sandberg and Adam Grant offers personal insights and research-based strategies for building resilience in the face of loss, grief, and adversity. It provides practical advice and inspiring stories that illustrate the power of resilience and the potential for growth in difficult times.

Exploring these resources can offer further inspiration and practical guidance for individuals seeking to cultivate resilience in their own lives.

Once Upon a time,

in the bustling city of New York, there lived a driven and ambitious woman named Elizabeth. As a high-powered executive in a prestigious corporation, Elizabeth's life was a whirlwind of meetings, deadlines, and endless responsibilities. She was constantly striving for success, working long hours, and neglecting her own well-being in the process.

One fateful day, while rushing to yet another important meeting, Elizabeth stumbled upon a small, quaint bookstore tucked away in a quiet corner of the city. Intrigued by the soothing atmosphere and the promise of respite from her hectic schedule, she decided to step inside.

As she perused the shelves, one book caught her eye: "The Art of Self-Care: Nurturing Your Mind, Body, and Spirit." Intrigued, she purchased the book and retreated to a cozy café nearby. With a steaming cup of herbal tea in hand, Elizabeth delved into the pages, eager to discover what lay within.

As she immersed herself in the words, Elizabeth felt a sense of awakening. The book spoke of the transformative power of self-care, urging her to prioritize her own well-being amidst the chaos of her demanding career. It emphasized that by nurturing her mind, body, and spirit, she could cultivate balance, resilience, and a deeper connection to herself.

Inspired by the book, Elizabeth decided to embark on a journey of self-discovery and well-being. She began by allocating time each morning to practice mindfulness meditation. With closed eyes and a focused mind, she learned to breathe deeply, quieting the relentless chatter and finding solace in the present moment. Through this practice, she found moments of clarity and a renewed sense of inner peace, allowing her to approach her work with greater focus and a calm demeanor.

Motivated by her newfound mental clarity, Elizabeth turned her attention to her physical well-being. She started attending early morning yoga classes, relishing the gentle stretches, and mindful movements that brought harmony to her body. The rhythmic flow of her practice awakened her senses and released the tension accumulated from long hours at her desk. She also made a conscious effort to nourish herself with wholesome, nutritious meals and prioritize restful sleep, recognizing that her body deserved care and rejuvenation.

However, Elizabeth yearned for something more—a deeper connection to her inner self and a sense of purpose beyond her corporate ambitions. The book guided her toward exploring her passions and interests outside of work. She enrolled in art classes, allowing her creativity to flourish on canvas. The strokes of color became an outlet for self-expression and a means of connecting with her deepest emotions.

In addition to artistic exploration, Elizabeth sought solace in nature. She discovered the power of a morning walk in the nearby park, surrounded by the vibrant hues of blooming flowers and the gentle rustle of leaves. This communion with nature brought her a profound sense of peace and connectedness, reminding her of the beauty and simplicity that existed beyond the concrete jungle.

As Elizabeth delved deeper into her self-care journey, she realized that setting healthy boundaries was crucial. She learned to prioritize her own needs and communicate her limits to colleagues and loved ones. This newfound assertiveness allowed her to carve out dedicated time for self-care without feeling guilty or overwhelmed.

With time, Elizabeth experienced the transformative benefits of her self-care practices. She noticed a newfound resilience within *herself—a willingness to embrace challenges with grace and poise. She became more attuned to her own desires and aspirations, pursuing personal projects and hobbies with enthusiasm and dedication. The once exhausted and overwhelmed executive had transformed into a confident, balanced, and empowered woman. Her transformation did not go unnoticed. Colleagues and friends marveled at her newfound radiance, seeking her advice on finding balance amidst the chaos of their own lives. Elizabeth became an advocate for self-care, sharing her story and encouraging others to embark on their own journeys of well-being.*

In the end, Elizabeth realized that self-care was not a luxury but a necessity. By nurturing her mind, body, and spirit, she had unlocked her true potential and found a deeper sense of fulfillment. Her commitment to self-care became a guiding light, illuminating a path of personal growth, happiness, and a profound connection to herself and the world around her.

Part V: Thriving Beyond Anxiety and Depression

In our journey towards emotional well-being, we encounter numerous hurdles, and among the most formidable are anxiety and depression. These conditions can cast a shadow over our lives, enveloping us in a seemingly endless cycle of worry, sadness, and despair. However, as we venture into Part V of our exploration, we begin to glimpse a glimmer of hope–a beacon guiding us towards a future where we not only survive but truly thrive beyond the clutches of anxiety and depression.

Thriving is a concept that transcends mere existence. It encapsulates a state of flourishing, resilience, and fulfillment that extends far beyond the absence of mental distress. It is a profound transformation, an evolution of the self that empowers us to embrace life's challenges, pursue our passions, and find purpose and meaning in our daily experiences. Thriving is not an unattainable ideal reserved for the fortunate few; it is a possibility within reach for all who are willing to embark on the path of growth and self-discovery.

In Part V, we embark on a journey that delves into the depths of our inner worlds, unraveling the intricacies of anxiety and depression, and exploring the pathways to liberation and transformation. We navigate the labyrinth of our thoughts, emotions, and behaviors, shining a light on the strategies, insights, and interventions that facilitate our ascent towards a life of thriving.

This section invites us to break free from the grip of anxiety, recognizing its nuanced manifestations, and equipping ourselves with practical tools to manage its influence. We explore the labyrinthine nature of worry, dissecting its origins and understanding its impact on our daily lives. We embrace evidence-based strategies that empower us to tame the worry monster, cultivate resilience, and foster a sense of inner calm and peace.

Simultaneously, we navigate the intricate landscape of depression, unraveling its complex web of emotions and cognitive distortions. We delve into the depths of understanding depression, unveiling its various types, symptoms, and diagnostic criteria. With this knowledge as our compass, we explore the terrain of coping with depression, uncovering the strategies, perspectives, and support systems that enable us to navigate the dark days and find the flickers of light amidst the shadows.

Beyond the exploration of anxiety and depression, we embark on a quest to nurture our holistic well-being. We recognize the importance of self-care—of nurturing our minds, bodies, and spirits with compassion and intention. We embrace the power of resilience, drawing inspiration from the experiences and wisdom of individuals who have triumphed over adversity and emerged stronger and wiser. We dive into the realm of therapeutic approaches, recognizing the transformative potential of professional help and treatment options, and the multitude of paths available for healing and growth.

Ultimately, Part V beckons us to a world where thriving is not a distant dream but a tangible reality—a world where anxiety and depression do not define us but instead become catalysts for personal growth, resilience, and purpose. Through introspection, understanding, and a commitment to our well-being, we discover that we possess the innate capacity to not only overcome our struggles but to rise above them and embrace a life of flourishing.

As we embark on this final leg of our transformative journey, let us kindle the flame of hope within our hearts, for it is hope that fuels our perseverance and propels us towards a future where anxiety and depression no longer hold sway. Together, let us unlock the secrets of thriving, embracing the full spectrum of our human experience, and cultivating a life of resilience, joy, and authentic fulfillment.

Embracing Positivity: Cultivating Joy and Gratitude

In a world often rife with challenges, uncertainty, and adversity, the pursuit of joy and gratitude may seem like an elusive endeavor. However, within the depths of our human experience lies a profound truth: that by intentionally cultivating positivity, we have the power to transform our lives and nourish our souls.

Joy, with its radiant essence, is a state of being that transcends mere happiness. It is a deep-seated contentment that arises from within, independent of external circumstances. It is not a fleeting emotion tied to momentary pleasures but a lasting sense of fulfillment that emanates from embracing the present moment and finding beauty in the simplest of things.

Cultivating joy requires a deliberate shift in perspective—a conscious choice to seek out the small miracles and everyday wonders that surround us. It beckons us to relinquish the weight of expectations and judgments, allowing us to embrace the raw beauty of life as it unfolds. Joy resides in the dance of laughter, the warmth of human connections, the awe-inspiring wonders of nature, and the fulfillment found in pursuing our passions.

Gratitude, like a gentle breeze, has the power to sweep away the cobwebs of negativity and nourish our souls. It is a profound acknowledgment of the blessings, big and small, that grace our lives. Gratitude is not a passive act of simply saying "thank you"; it is an active practice of recognizing and appreciating the abundance that surrounds us.

When we cultivate gratitude, we shift our focus from what is lacking to what is present. It is a transformative lens through which we view the world, allowing us to find meaning and beauty even in the face of adversity. Gratitude opens our hearts to the interconnectedness of all things, fostering a sense of humility, compassion, and appreciation for the tapestry of life.

To embrace positivity and cultivate joy and gratitude, we must first develop awareness. We become mindful observers of our thoughts, emotions, and attitudes, gently redirecting our attention towards the aspects of life that uplift and inspire us. We train ourselves to notice the small moments of joy that often go unnoticed—the soft glow of a sunrise, the laughter of a loved one, the kind gesture of a stranger.

Practicing gratitude involves intentionally reflecting on the blessings in our lives. It may take the form of keeping a gratitude journal, where we regularly write down the things we are grateful for. It may involve expressing gratitude to others, acknowledging their contributions and impact on our lives. It may even extend to acts of kindness, as we seek to bring joy and gratitude to others.

Famous psychologist Dr. Martin Seligman, a pioneer in positive psychology, advocates for the cultivation of positive emotions as a pathway to well-being. His research highlights the power of gratitude and the intentional pursuit of joy in fostering happiness and overall life satisfaction. Drawing inspiration from his work, we can understand that embracing positivity is not a trivial pursuit but a profound commitment to our well-being.

As we embark on the journey of embracing positivity, let us remember that it is not a one-time accomplishment but a lifelong practice. It requires patience, self-compassion, and a willingness to let go of negativity and embrace the inherent goodness within ourselves and the world. It is a journey of self-discovery and self-transformation, where each step forward brings us closer to the vibrant tapestry of joy and gratitude that awaits us.

In this pursuit, we must also recognize that embracing positivity does not negate the existence of pain, sorrow, or difficult emotions. Rather, it invites us to hold space for the full spectrum of human experiences, acknowledging that even within the darkest moments, there is room for growth, resilience, and the seeds of joy and gratitude to take root.

As we navigate life's twists and turns, let us embark on the path of embracing positivity–a path that leads us to the profound realization that within our hearts, we hold the power to cultivate joy, gratitude, and a deep sense of fulfillment. Through mindful awareness, intentional practices, and a shift in perspective, we unlock the door to a life imbued with radiant joy, unwavering gratitude, and an unwavering appreciation for the richness of our existence.

Here are some examples of how individuals can embrace positivity and cultivate joy and gratitude in their lives:

Practicing Mindfulness: Engaging in mindfulness meditation or mindful living can help individuals develop awareness of the present moment and cultivate a sense of gratitude for the simple pleasures in life. It involves observing thoughts and emotions without judgment and fully immersing oneself in the present experience.

Keeping a Gratitude Journal: Setting aside a few minutes each day to write down things for which one is grateful can shift the focus towards positive aspects of life. It may include expressing appreciation for supportive relationships, moments of joy, personal achievements, or even the beauty of nature. Regularly revisiting the gratitude journal can serve as a reminder of the abundance in one's life.

Acts of Kindness: Engaging in acts of kindness towards others not only brings joy to those receiving but also cultivates a sense of fulfillment and gratitude within oneself. Acts of kindness can be as simple as offering a helping hand to someone in need, volunteering for a charitable cause, or expressing kindness and compassion in daily interactions.

Finding Joy in Simple Pleasures: Embracing and savoring the small moments of joy in everyday life can significantly contribute to overall well-being. It may involve taking a walk in nature, enjoying a delicious meal, spending quality time with loved ones, or engaging in hobbies and activities that bring a sense of joy and fulfillment.

Shifting Perspectives: Actively challenging negative thoughts and reframing them in a more positive light can help cultivate a mindset of gratitude and joy. This involves consciously choosing to focus on the silver linings, finding lessons in difficult situations, and embracing a mindset of growth and resilience.

Cultivating Positive Relationships: Surrounding oneself with positive and supportive individuals can contribute to a sense of joy and gratitude. Nurturing healthy relationships, expressing appreciation for loved ones, and fostering connections that uplift and inspire can create an environment conducive to positivity.

Engaging in Self-Care: Prioritizing self-care practices that nourish the mind, body, and spirit is essential for cultivating joy and gratitude. This may include activities such as practicing self-compassion, engaging in regular exercise, getting sufficient rest, pursuing hobbies and interests, and engaging in activities that bring joy and fulfillment.

Embracing the Power of Positive Affirmations: Utilizing positive affirmations can help rewire negative thought patterns and cultivate a more optimistic mindset. Affirmations such as "I am grateful for the abundance in my life" or "I choose joy in every moment" can help shift focus towards positivity and foster a sense of gratitude and joy.

By incorporating these practices into daily life, individuals can actively embrace positivity, cultivate joy, and nurture a deep sense of gratitude. While the journey may require commitment and practice, the rewards of a more joyful and grateful existence are immeasurable.

Strengthening Relationships: Finding Support in Your Journey

Human beings are inherently social creatures, wired to seek connection, support, and understanding from others. In our journey through life, the quality of our relationships plays a pivotal role in our overall well-being and personal growth. When faced with the challenges of anxiety, depression, or any other emotional struggles, having a strong support system becomes even more crucial.

The power of relationships lies in their ability to provide solace, encouragement, and a safe space for vulnerability. They can serve as beacons of light during the darkest of times, offering companionship and a sense of belonging. When we forge deep and meaningful connections, we tap into a wellspring of strength that can help us navigate the complexities of our inner worlds.

Building and nurturing supportive relationships is a multifaceted process that requires intention, effort, and vulnerability. It starts with cultivating self-awareness and understanding our own needs and boundaries. By knowing ourselves, we can better communicate our needs to others, fostering healthier and more fulfilling connections.

Authentic communication is the cornerstone of strong relationships. It involves not only expressing our own emotions and thoughts honestly but also actively listening and empathizing with others. When we feel heard and validated, and when we extend the same to others, the bonds of trust and understanding grow stronger.

Famous psychologists such as Carl Rogers and John Bowlby have emphasized the significance of secure attachments and supportive relationships in human development. They have highlighted the importance of empathy, active listening, and unconditional positive regard in fostering healthy connections. Their research underscores the profound impact that supportive relationships can have on our emotional well-being and personal growth.

In our journey to strengthen relationships, it is essential to foster a culture of compassion and empathy. We can seek to understand the experiences, perspectives, and emotions of others without judgment. By practicing empathy, we create an environment that promotes open and honest communication, deepening our connections and nurturing a sense of support.

Vulnerability is a key ingredient in building strong relationships. It requires us to shed the armor of self-protection and bravely share our fears, struggles, and insecurities with trusted individuals. When we allow ourselves to be vulnerable, we invite others to do the same, forging deeper connections based on authenticity and mutual understanding.

Support can come in various forms, depending on the unique needs and preferences of individuals. It may involve seeking professional help from therapists, counselors, or support groups. These resources provide a safe and nonjudgmental space where individuals can explore their emotions, gain insights, and receive guidance tailored to their specific circumstances.

Additionally, friends and family members can play an invaluable role in our support system. Their unwavering presence, love, and encouragement can provide a lifeline during difficult times. By nurturing these relationships, we create a network of support that strengthens our resilience and helps us weather life's storms.

In the digital age, technology offers new avenues for connection and support. Online communities, forums, and social media platforms provide spaces where individuals can find like-minded individuals, share their experiences, and receive support and validation. However, it is important to approach online interactions with discernment and ensure the sources of support are reliable and reputable.

Strengthening relationships and finding support in our journey requires an ongoing commitment. It involves giving and receiving, offering support to others while also being open to receiving support when needed. It requires cultivating empathy, practicing active listening, and prioritizing quality time spent with loved ones.

By nurturing our relationships and finding support in our journey, we create a safety net that uplifts us during challenging times and celebrates our triumphs. We tap into a wellspring of strength and resilience, knowing that we are not alone in our struggles. Through the power of connection and support, we find solace, inspiration, and the courage to continue growing, healing, and thriving.

Once upon a time,

in a bustling city filled with endless possibilities, there lived a young woman named Maya. From the outside, Maya seemed to have it all together—her vibrant smile, impeccable style, and successful career masked the battles she fought within. Maya carried the weight of anxiety and depression, like a heavy cloak draped over her shoulders. Each day felt like an uphill climb, and the world around her seemed to move at a relentless pace. The constant worry and the persistent cloud of sadness cast shadows on her dreams and aspirations.

Like many, Maya yearned for a life free from the suffocating grip of anxiety and depression. She longed to find peace, fulfillment, and the courage to pursue her passions with unwavering confidence. And so, she embarked on a deeply personal journey of self-discovery and healing.

Maya sought solace in the pages of books and articles, devouring the stories of others who had walked a similar path. She found inspiration in the writings of renowned psychologists like Carl Jung and Viktor Frankl, who spoke of the power of inner strength and resilience in the face of adversity. Their words resonated deep within her soul, igniting a flicker of hope.

In her quest for healing, Maya turned to therapy—a safe haven where she could unravel the complexities of her emotions and confront the roots of her struggles. With the guidance of her empathetic therapist, Dr. Rodriguez, Maya delved into the depths of her past, unearthing buried traumas and addressing the deeply ingrained negative beliefs that held her back.

Through therapy, Maya learned that she was not alone in her battles. She discovered a supportive community of individuals who had also experienced the weight of anxiety and depression. In support groups and online forums, she connected with kindred spirits who shared their stories, their triumphs, and their setbacks. In their shared vulnerability, Maya found solace and a profound sense of belonging.

Maya realized that healing was not a linear process but a journey of self-compassion and self-discovery. She embraced mindfulness and meditation, practices that anchored her in the present moment and allowed her to observe her thoughts and emotions with gentle curiosity. In these moments of stillness, she began to cultivate a deep sense of self-awareness and acceptance.
As Maya continued to navigate her journey, she understood the importance of self-care and nurturing her mind, body, and spirit. She prioritized restorative activities that brought her joy— painting, dancing, spending time in nature, and connecting with loved ones. She learned to set boundaries, saying no to things that drained her energy and yes to experiences that nourished her soul. But perhaps the most transformative aspect of Maya's journey was the strengthening of her relationships. She opened up to her closest friends and family, sharing her fears and vulnerabilities. In return, they embraced her with unconditional love and support. Through their presence, Maya realized that vulnerability was not a weakness but a doorway to deeper connections and authentic relationships.

Over time, Maya's once-heavy cloak of anxiety and depression began to lighten. She noticed moments of genuine laughter, a renewed sense of purpose, and an appreciation for the beauty in everyday life. Maya became an advocate for mental health, sharing her story with others who yearned to break free from the chains of anxiety and depression.

Maya's journey serves as a reminder that each of us has the strength within to embark on a path of healing and transformation. Her story resonates with those who have felt the weight of anxiety and depression, inviting them to embrace their own unique journey of self-discovery and growth. Maya's tale reminds us that there is hope, that there is a way to thrive beyond the darkness and step into a life of authenticity, joy, and fulfillment.

Embracing a Meaningful Life: Setting Goals and Pursuing Passion

Life is a tapestry of moments, experiences, and choices. We all yearn for a life that is not only filled with happiness and contentment but also imbued with purpose and meaning. In our quest to find fulfillment, setting goals and pursuing our passions becomes an integral part of the journey.

Setting goals allows us to chart a course for our lives, to define the direction we want to take and the milestones we aim to achieve. Goals provide us with a sense of purpose, a sense of striving towards something greater than ourselves. They give us a roadmap, guiding us through the twists and turns of life, and offering a sense of fulfillment when we reach our desired destinations.

Meaningful goals are those that align with our values, passions, and aspirations. They reflect our authentic selves and ignite a fire within us, propelling us forward even in the face of obstacles. When we set goals that are deeply connected to our core values, we create a sense of alignment and harmony in our lives, fostering a deep sense of fulfillment.

Psychologist Abraham Maslow's famous hierarchy of needs highlights the significance of self-actualization–a stage where individuals strive to fulfill their highest potential and lead a life of purpose. Setting and pursuing meaningful goals is an essential component of this self-actualization process. It allows us to tap into our unique talents, strengths, and passions, and to contribute to the world in a way that is personally fulfilling and impactful.

In the pursuit of meaningful goals, it is essential to adopt a growth mindset–a mindset that embraces challenges, views setbacks as opportunities for learning, and believes in the power of effort and perseverance. A growth mindset recognizes that the journey towards our goals is not always smooth, but it is through overcoming obstacles that we gain resilience, wisdom, and personal growth.

Passion, in its purest form, is the driving force behind the pursuit of meaningful goals. It is the spark that ignites our souls, infusing our actions with enthusiasm, energy, and dedication. When we align our goals with our passions, our efforts become purposeful, and the path we tread becomes a source of joy and fulfillment.

Finding and pursuing our passions requires introspection and exploration. It involves reflecting on our interests, curiosities, and the activities that bring us a sense of flow—a state of being fully immersed and engaged in what we are doing. It may involve trying new experiences, stepping outside of our comfort zones, and embracing uncertainty. Through this journey of self-discovery, we unearth the passions that will fuel our pursuit of a meaningful life.

However, it is important to note that the pursuit of meaningful goals should not be driven solely by external measures of success or societal expectations. True fulfillment lies in setting goals that are aligned with our authentic selves, not those dictated by others. It requires us to define success on our own terms and to embrace the uniqueness of our own journey.

In the pursuit of a meaningful life, it is also essential to cultivate balance and self-care. While goals and passions drive us forward, it is crucial to nurture our well-being along the way. This may involve creating space for rest, relaxation, and self-reflection. It may mean establishing healthy boundaries, saying no to commitments that drain our energy, and prioritizing our physical and emotional health.

Ultimately, embracing a meaningful life is about weaving together our goals, passions, values, and self-care into a harmonious tapestry. It is about finding purpose and fulfillment in every aspect of our existence. As we set goals and pursue our passions, we embark on a transformative journey—one that allows us to leave a lasting impact on ourselves, others, and the world around us.

In the words of psychologist Mihaly Csikszentmihalyi, "The best moments in our lives are not the passive, receptive, relaxing times... The best moments usually occur if a person's body or mind is stretched to its limits in a voluntary effort to accomplish something difficult and worthwhile." So let us embark on this journey of embracing a meaningful life, setting goals that resonate with our deepest selves, and pursuing our passions with unwavering determination. In doing so, we unlock the door to a life of purpose, fulfillment, and joy.

Finding Light and Empowering Transformation

As we come to the end of this transformative journey, we are reminded of the indomitable human spirit, the power within each of us to rise above the challenges that life presents. Throughout the exploration of anxiety, depression, resilience, and personal growth, we have discovered that there is light even in the darkest corners of our existence.

Anxiety and depression may cast their shadows upon us, but we have learned that they do not define us. Through understanding, recognition, and self-compassion, we can shed light on these internal struggles and begin to take steps towards healing and recovery. We have uncovered the importance of seeking professional help, embracing therapeutic approaches, and cultivating resilience as we navigate the complexities of our minds and emotions.

In our quest for a meaningful life, we have delved into the depths of our souls, uncovering our passions, values, and aspirations. We have witnessed the transformative power of setting meaningful goals that align with our authentic selves, and we have embraced the pursuit of these goals with unwavering determination. Along the way, we have discovered the significance of self-care, nurturing our minds, bodies, and spirits, as we strive for balance and well-being.

Throughout this journey, we have not walked alone. We have found solace and strength in the support of our loved ones, our communities, and the wisdom of renowned psychologists who have illuminated our path. From Carl Jung's exploration of the depths of the human psyche to Viktor Frankl's profound insights on finding meaning in the face of adversity, their words have resonated with us, guiding us towards self-discovery and empowerment.

As we reflect upon the lessons learned and the transformations experienced, we realize that this journey is not a destination but a lifelong commitment to growth, self-compassion, and the pursuit of a meaningful life. We understand that thriving beyond anxiety and depression is not an endpoint, but a continuous process of self-care, self-reflection, and embracing the power of positivity.

In embracing a life of light and empowerment, we recognize that challenges may still arise, but we have the tools and the resilience to overcome them. We have cultivated a mindset that views obstacles as opportunities for growth, and we approach life with gratitude, joy, and a deep sense of purpose. We understand that our stories are still being written, and we have the power to shape our narratives with courage, authenticity, and unwavering determination.

So, as we step into the world beyond these pages, let us carry with us the lessons learned and the transformations experienced. Let us continue to nurture our minds, bodies, and spirits, to embrace the power of self-care, and to pursue our passions with unwavering dedication. Together, we can create a ripple effect of positive change, inspiring others to embark on their own journeys of self-discovery, healing, and empowerment.

In the end, it is our collective journey, our resilience, and our unwavering commitment to growth that will illuminate the path for others. Let us find light in the darkest of moments and empower transformation in ourselves and those around us. For we are the authors of our stories, and together, we can create a world where anxiety and depression are met with empathy, understanding, and hope.

References

- *American Psychological Association (APA): The APA is a widely recognized organization in the field of psychology, offering valuable resources, research articles, and information on various mental health topics. Their website is a great starting point for exploring anxiety, depression, resilience, and therapeutic approaches. You can visit their website at www.apa.org.*
- *National Institute of Mental Health (NIMH): As part of the U.S. Department of Health and Human Services, NIMH is a leading research institution focused on mental health disorders. Their website provides evidence-based information, research updates, and resources related to anxiety, depression, and various treatment options. Visit their website at www.nimh.nih.gov.*
- *"The Anxiety and Phobia Workbook" by Edmund J. Bourne: This book is a comprehensive resource for understanding and managing anxiety disorders. It offers practical strategies, exercises, and insights into different types of anxiety disorders, their symptoms, and treatment approaches. It is widely recommended by mental health professionals.*
- *"The Upward Spiral: Using Neuroscience to Reverse the Course of Depression, One Small Change at a Time" by Alex Korb: This book explores the neuroscience behind depression and provides practical strategies for managing and overcoming depressive symptoms. It offers a unique perspective on how small changes in our thoughts, behaviors, and lifestyle can have a significant impact on our well-being.*
- *"Man's Search for Meaning" by Viktor E. Frankl: This seminal work by Viktor Frankl, an esteemed psychiatrist and Holocaust survivor, explores the search for meaning and purpose in life. It offers profound insights into the human capacity to find meaning even in the most challenging circumstances.*
- *"Resilience: The Science of Mastering Life's Greatest Challenges" by Steven M. Southwick and Dennis S. Charney: This book delves into the concept of resilience and provides evidence-based strategies for building resilience and overcoming adversity. It draws from scientific research, real-life examples, and expert perspectives.*
- *Please note that while these sources are reputable, it's always a good idea to cross-reference information and consult multiple sources to gain a comprehensive understanding of the topics discussed.*

About the Author

Mr. Raul Dominguez, MIO Psych, is an esteemed IO Psychologist who has made notable contributions to understanding abnormal behavior. With a passion for supporting mental health, he combines his expertise in organizational dynamics with insights into anxiety and depression. In his book, "Finding Light in the Darkness: A Guide to Overcoming Anxiety and Depression," Mr. Dominguez offers a compassionate and informed perspective, empowering readers on their path to well-being.